The Comparable Worth Controversy

HENRY J. AARON and CAMERAN M. LOUGY

The Comparable Worth Controversy

THE BROOKINGS INSTITUTION
Washington, D.C.

THE BROOKINGS INSTITUTION
1775 Massachusetts Avenue, N.W., Washington, D.C. 20036

Library of Congress Cataloging-in-Publication data:

Aaron, Henry J.
The comparable worth controversy.
Includes index.
1. Pay equity—United States. 2. Equal pay for equal work—United States. I. Lougy, Cameran, 1963–
II. Title
HD6061.2.U6A37 1986 331.2′1 85-48206

ISBN 0-8157-0041-5 (pbk.)

1 2 3 4 5 6 7 8 9

THE BROOKINGS INSTITUTION is an independent organization devoted to nonpartisan research, education, and publication in economics, government, foreign policy, and the social sciences generally. Its principal purposes are to aid in the development of sound public policies and to promote public understanding of issues of national importance.

The Institution was founded on December 8, 1927, to merge the activities of the Institute for Government Research, founded in 1916, the Institute of Economics, founded in 1922, and the Robert Brookings Graduate School of Economics and Government, founded in 1924.

The Board of Trustees is responsible for the general administration of the Institution, while the immediate direction of the policies, program, and staff is vested in the President, assisted by an advisory committee of the officers and staff. The by-laws of the Institution state: "It is the function of the Trustees to make possible the conduct of scientific research, and publication, under the most favorable conditions, and to safeguard the independence of the research staff in the pursuit of their studies and in the publication of the results of such studies. It is not a part of their function to determine, control, or influence the conduct of particular investigations or the conclusions reached."

The President bears final responsibility for the decision to publish a manuscript as a Brookings book. In reaching his judgment on the competence, accuracy, and objectivity of each study, the President is advised by the director of the appropriate research program and weighs the views of a panel of expert outside readers who report to him in confidence on the quality of the work. Publication of a work signifies that it is deemed a competent treatment worthy of public consideration but does not imply endorsement of conclusions or recommendations.

The Institution maintains its position of neutrality on issues of public policy in order to safeguard the intellectual freedom of the staff. Hence interpretations or conclusions in Brookings publications should be understood to be solely those of the authors and should not be attributed to the Institution, to its trustees, officers, or other staff members, or to the organizations that support its research.

Foreword

WHAT, if anything, should be done to close the gap between the earnings of women and men? For those who believe that pay tends to reflect productivity and working conditions, the current pay differential simply reflects the operation of market forces. According to this view, to receive improved relative pay women must choose different lines of work and stay in the paid labor force longer without interruption. Others, however, argue that the relative pay of women is affected significantly by prejudice or tradition and that it should be increased by administrative or judicial action. One method of increasing the relative pay for jobs filled predominantly by women is to adjust wages on the basis of job evaluations. According to this approach, holders of jobs judged to have comparable worth should receive equal pay, whether or not the current market wages are identical.

In this book Henry J. Aaron and Cameran M. Lougy examine the controversy that has arisen around the proposal to adjust wages based on the principle of comparable worth. They conclude that proponents have overrated the potential benefits from such adjustments and that opponents have exaggerated the risks. They are persuaded that women have suffered from labor market discrimination, which accounts for part of the male-female wage gap. But much of this discrimination affects aspects of labor market behavior that even a resolute application of wage adjustments based on comparable worth could not change. Application of comparable worth in the public sector and collectively bargained wage settlements in the private sector could improve the pay of women workers, and there is little evidence that such adjustments would reduce overall economic efficiency. However, efforts to require private-sector employers to implement comparable worth would embroil the courts in numerous administrative disputes, which they would be poorly qualified to settle in volume. The authors propose instead a more cautious and limited procedure for implementing wage adjustments.

Henry J. Aaron is a senior fellow in the Brookings Economic Studies program and professor of economics at the University of Maryland. Cameran M. Lougy, formerly a research assistant in the Brookings Economic Studies program, is a graduate student at the Woodrow Wilson School of Public and International Affairs at Princeton University.

The authors thank Katharine G. Abraham, Gary T. Burtless, Suzanne Donovan, Heidi I. Hartmann, Mark R. Killingsworth, June A. O'Neill, Alice M. Rivlin, Steven H. Sandell, and Isabel V. Sawhill for helpful criticism on early drafts. Helen Remick at the University of Washington supplied data on job evaluation point scores from the state of Washington. Lori R. Grunin provided research assistance. Nancy Davidson edited the manuscript; Carolyn Rutsch and Almaz Zelleke checked it for factual accuracy; and Max Franke prepared the index.

The views expressed in this book are those of the authors and should not be ascribed to the trustees, officers, or other staff members of the Brookings Institution.

BRUCE K. MACLAURY
President

July 1986
Washington, D.C.

Contents

The Comparable Worth Controversy

WHY do women earn less than men, and what should be done about it? How one approaches these two questions depends a great deal on one's view about how wages are determined.

According to one view, most of the difference between men's and women's earnings is attributable to decisions that women freely make—about how much to work, what occupations to choose, and when to leave or enter the labor force. According to this "efficient labor market" view, women earn relatively little because they have chosen jobs that happen to have low productivity and low wages, that permit them to enter or leave the work force, that require relatively little training, or that are not dangerous or onerous. This view holds that because labor markets function efficiently and fairly wages reflect productivity and compensate workers for taking difficult or dangerous assignments. It also holds that employers have little incentive to discriminate against women (or any other group) and have strong incentives to use workers, regardless of sex, where they are most productive. According to this view, women will be paid as well as men when, but only when, they acquire similar training, enter similar occupations, and remain in jobs without time out for other activities such as child rearing.

A second view holds that wages in different jobs and occupations are influenced strongly by custom and tradition. According to this "institutional" view, jobs requiring similar skills, contributing similar amounts to employer revenues, and having similar working conditions may be paid quite differently because of habit, tradition, or discrimination. This view acknowledges the contention, held by believers in the efficient labor market, that women could improve their relative earnings by trying to enter jobs traditionally held by men or by pursuing careers as single-mindedly as men do. But this view holds that progress would be slow, both because men would resist the entry of women into previously male-dominated activities and because wage differentials in female-dominated jobs could persist indefinitely even if they are not founded on job or worker characteristics relevant to job performance.

According to the efficient labor market view, efforts by the government to reduce the male-female wage gap would probably hurt women and would certainly reduce overall economic efficiency. Boosting wages artificially would cause employers to hire fewer women. The result would be higher wages for women who kept their jobs, but fewer jobs of the kinds traditionally filled by women. Overall economic efficiency would be reduced because people would be prevented from working where their productivity was highest, given their preferences for working conditions.

According to the institutional view, women's earnings can be increased in a variety of ways. Employers can be persuaded or compelled to accept women in previously all-male jobs, or wages can be equalized in jobs held predominantly by either sex and evaluated as similar. This latter approach to increasing the relative earnings of women has become known as "comparable worth."

Under this approach, expert panels would evaluate the intellectual and physical demands of jobs within a particular company or controlled by a single employer (such as a state or local government). The panels would assign points to each job based on its working conditions, responsibility, and other characteristics, and would weight each of these factors. The result would be a composite score or index that, it is claimed, measures the "worth" of each job. People holding jobs of comparable worth as measured by these scores would receive equal pay.

Past applications of this method generally reveal that incumbents in jobs filled primarily by women are paid less than those in jobs with equal scores filled primarily by men. Thus setting pay on the basis of these scores would raise women's wages relative to men's. This procedure is the essence of the movement to set pay for various jobs according to their comparable worth. It is one of several methods that can be used for countering sex-based discrimination.[1]

Comparable worth, it should be noted, is usually determined on the

1. In principle, similar methods could be used for adjusting wages among groups defined by characteristics other than sex if such wage differences were attributable to discrimination.

basis of job attributes, not on the characteristics of their incumbents.[2] The comparable worth movement seeks to promote the use of job evaluations as the basis for determining pay in both the private and public sectors. Supporters claim that this method of setting wages is an important tool for advancing pay equity. Indeed, the terms "comparable worth" and "pay equity" are often used interchangeably, although opponents of comparable worth often embrace the goal of pay equity but reject comparable worth as a strategy to achieve that goal. They claim that job evaluations are inherently arbitrary and the resulting pay scales have no claim to fairness. Some assert that trying to set pay in this way is an insidious attack on free markets and economic competition.

Unfortunately for those who try to make sense of these conflicting claims, supporters and opponents of comparable worth frequently seem to be talking about different things, as table 1 indicates. Table 1 does not fully characterize the views of many participants in the debate, but it does represent the core views. One of the key issues is whether comparable worth would be implemented in both the public and private sectors. Opponents suggest that it must entail the mandatory setting of wages in both sectors according to job evaluations. Many proponents hold that private-sector wages can be set through collective bargaining and other market forces. Supporters do not agree among themselves on whether acceptance of the principles of comparable worth requires intervention in private wage setting by the courts or government officials. Opponents assume that such intervention would occur. In general, opponents of comparable worth foresee far larger departures from current business and economic procedures than do supporters.

Both proponents and opponents of comparable worth view it as only one of a menu of techniques for dealing with labor market discrimination. Other techniques include private litigation under title VII of the Civil Rights Act of 1964 or the Equal Pay Act of 1963, affirmative action to achieve goals for hiring or advancement of women, and regulations by the Office of Federal Contract Compliance Programs of the Department of Labor.

Because supporters of comparable worth claim to be advocating one

2. For a notable exception, see Barbara R. Bergmann, "The Economic Case for Comparable Worth," in Heidi I. Hartmann, ed., *Comparable Worth: New Directions for Research* (Washington, D.C.: National Academy Press, 1985), pp. 71–85.

Table 1. *Modal Views of Supporters and Opponents of Comparable Worth*

Point of disagreement	*Views of supporters*	*Views of opponents*
Wage gap	Women earn about 60–65 percent of what men earn.	No disagreement.
Explanation of wage gap	Part of the gap disappears if one adjusts for hours, more for factors such as education, age. The remainder is evidence of discrimination.	About half the gap can be explained statistically. One should adjust not only for hours, but for experience and time spent outside labor force. Difference is about half as large for young workers. The remainder may be a measure of female preferences for certain jobs or a measure of the investigator's ignorance, but not necessarily of discrimination.
How labor markets work	Institutional factors are important in wage setting; internal labor markets are used in hiring and promotion; women are crowded into certain occupations. Supply and demand and wage flexibility play small role. There is little tendency for competition to eliminate discrimination.	Wages are determined primarily by supply and demand; wages are flexible and labor markets adjust so that supply equals demand. The goal of maximizing profits leads employers to eliminate discrimination.
Role of job evaluation in setting wages	Job evaluation based on job characteristics can measure value of various jobs to employers; it can establish ordinal, if not cardinal, ranking of job values.	Job evaluation is inherently subjective. The only reliable indicator of the value of a job is the wage an employer is willing to pay a person to fill it.

What comparable worth entails	It will be applied on a firm-by-firm basis. It will be used in union organizing and collective bargaining. In public sector, job evaluation studies would be routinely used in setting wages. In private sector, job evaluation would be promoted and would form the basis for comparable worth adjustments. Private employers who do job evaluation studies must follow them.	Mandatory job evaluation in both public and private sectors, possibly economywide. New legislation or court interpretation of existing law authorizing wholesale intervention by executive agencies (regulation) or courts (litigation) in wage setting would abridge freedom of employers to set wages, alone or through collective bargaining, subject to market discipline.
Effects of comparable worth	Significant changes in relative wages of jobs, but small overall effect on wage costs (even if equalization is through leveling up). Little job displacement. Little effect on economic efficiency. Cost of eliminating discrimination is never a valid excuse for inaction. It will decrease segregation because higher wages in traditionally female jobs will encourage men to move in.	Large increases in wages of millions of jobs, with great overall cost. Major reduction in economic efficiency and increase in prices. Major disemployment effects, especially for low-wage unskilled workers. It will increase segregation because higher wages in traditionally female jobs will discourage women from moving out.

thing and opponents seem to be criticizing another, the verbal exchange between them frequently confuses rather than enlightens. The tone of the exchanges heightens the problem. For example, Michael Levin attributes support of comparable worth to "rage at all differences in the basic role of the sexes," and Michael Brody alleges that comparable worth supporters harbor a "bewildered hatred for the whole idea of labor markets" and have "an elitist contempt—the contempt of Ivy League women with sociology degrees—for the ordinary working stiffs."[3] While one may admire the power of such assertions to rally the already persuaded, they do little to illuminate the issues.

We shall try here to explain briefly and simply what the debate is all about. We begin by reviewing the evidence on how much, if any, of the discrepancy between male and female earnings results from labor market discrimination. We then explain the quite discrepant views that supporters and opponents of comparable worth typically hold on how labor markets work. To clarify how comparable worth would operate, we explain the workings and current application of job evaluation methods. We then examine the claims made by supporters and opponents of comparable worth of its economic effects and compare comparable worth with other methods of dealing with labor market discrimination. Our major conclusions are:

—Half or more of the difference between male and female earnings can be explained by factors unrelated to any possible discrimination by individual employers. Some of the remainder of the gap is attributable to patterns of behavior by employers and employees that may reflect either discrimination or perfectly acceptable voluntary behavior. Some is attributable to discrimination, but we are unsure how much. And part of the gap is unexplained. Statistical evidence can never prove, but only suggest, that the male-female wage gap is caused by discrimination. However, there is considerable evidence—including suggestive statistical analyses, surveys and small controlled experiments, anecdotes, and past litigation—all of which strongly suggest the past prevalence and lingering importance of such discrimination.

—Competitive labor markets sometimes combat discrimination, but they cannot be relied upon to do so. Factors other than the supply of

3. Michael Levin, "Comparable Worth: The Feminist Road to Socialism," *Commentary*, vol. 78 (September 1984), p. 16; and Michael Brody, "New Era in Pay Scales? The Push for 'Comparable Worth' Could Destroy the Job Market," *Barron's*, November 21, 1983.

workers or their productivity play a major role in job assignment, wage setting, and promotion for extended periods of time.

—Job evaluation and wage setting according to job characteristics are inherently arbitrary, in the sense that the resulting scores may or may not be closely related to worker productivity or to diverse judgments about the attractiveness of different occupations. But employers often use job evaluation when objective evidence on productivity is costly or impossible to obtain, and unions support it.

—Courts should continue to use the results of job evaluation studies as one piece of evidence in determining whether labor market discrimination exists. They should not require that wages be set according to the results of such studies, however, because different equally defensible estimates will rank jobs differently or will indicate widely varying wage adjustments.[4]

—The use of such job evaluation techniques in the public sector is one of many reasonable bases for setting public-sector wages.

—The rationale for comparable worth fits well within arguments traditionally used by union organizers to recruit new union members. The use of comparable worth arguments in both private- and public-sector union organizing and collective bargaining is simply the application of old methods in a new environment.

—Application of comparable worth in public-sector wage setting or through collective bargaining in the private sector is likely to reduce slightly the discrepancy between male and female earnings. Comparable worth would indirectly affect the male-female earnings gap by encouraging employers to think about relative pay in cases where they enjoy discretion.

—While wage adjustments based on evaluations of comparable worth can correct some forms of labor market discrimination, they are simply irrelevant to others—for example, where women are denied entry to particular jobs or promotions that they merit. In such cases available remedies other than comparable worth must be used. For that reason, affirmative action and civil rights litigation based on other arguments offer at least as much promise for improving the labor market status of women as would even the most expansive acceptance of wage adjustments based on comparable worth.

4. An important question currently before the courts concerns whether employers who use job evaluations should be required to use them in setting wages. This issue is addressed below.

—Widespread increases in real wages of women through comparable worth adjustments would slightly increase aggregate wage growth over several years. The consequence, adverse for some women, would be reduced employment of women in some traditionally female jobs.

—Application of comparable worth could increase or decrease overall economic efficiency; there is simply no way to tell.

Our major conclusion is that the intensity of rhetoric lavished on the issue of comparable worth is grossly excessive. Where labor market discrimination against women can be demonstrated, comparable worth is only one of several remedies and often neither the most relevant nor the most powerful. Comparable worth is neither a panacea nor a Trojan horse threatening free enterprise capitalism. Like most ideas, it can be driven to extremes. If applied in a limited way, it holds some promise for offsetting a small part of the effects of discrimination on women's earnings.[5]

Male and Female Earnings: The Facts and What They Mean

Women earn much less than men do. The gap is larger for the old than for the young. The table below shows that in 1984 median weekly earnings of women averaged 35.2 percent less than those of men.[6] The gap between female and male hourly earnings is somewhat smaller—about 30 percent—because women on full-time schedules, on the average, work about 8 percent fewer hours per week than men on full-time schedules do.[7]

Age	*Ratio of female to male earnings*
16–24	87.5
25–34	74.0
35–44	62.4
45–54	59.8
55–64	59.9
65 and over	66.4
All ages	64.8

5. Paul Weiler reaches similar conclusions to those stated here in "The Uses and the Limits of Comparable Worth in the Pursuit of Pay Equity for Women" (Harvard Law School, October 1985).

6. U.S. Department of Labor, Bureau of Labor Statistics, *Employment and Earnings*, vol. 32 (January 1985), p. 210.

7. Ibid., p. 42.

Table 2. *Average Hourly Earnings among Industries, by Proportion of Workers Who Are Women*

Proportion of workers in industry who are women (percent)	*Number of male workers (thousands)*	*Number of female workers (thousands)*	*Average hourly earnings in industry (dollars)*
70 and over	2,057.9	7,475.5	5.71
50–69.9	4,693.1	6,931.5	6.08
40–49.9	7,634.3	5,815.5	7.58
30–39.9	1,880.3	954.9	8.15
20–29.9	9,938.1	3,301.0	8.34
10–19.9	8,793.9	1,671.1	9.53
0–9.9	3,228.9	292.7	11.56

Source: Authors' calculations based on Janet L. Norwood, *The Female-Male Earnings Gap: A Review of Employment and Earnings Issues,* U.S. Department of Labor, Bureau of Labor Statistics, Report 673 (Government Printing Office, September 1982), table 4; based on July 1982 averages.

The industrial and occupational segregation of men and women is even more striking than the wage differences. The narrower the definition of industries and occupations, the greater the apparent segregation. According to Department of Labor classifications, in July 1982, 37 percent of all women worked in industries in which at least 65 percent of the employees were women.[8] Furthermore, the larger the proportion of female workers, the lower the average hourly wage (see table 2).

Segregation by occupation is even greater than segregation by industry. Furthermore, men and women performing similar tasks are often employed in establishments that hire workers predominantly of one sex. Among 427 occupational classes, 80 percent of women work in occupations in which at least 70 percent of the employees are women.[9] A study of a sample of 393 companies in California found that only 10 percent of all employees worked in establishment job categories that had both

8. Janet L. Norwood, *The Female-Male Earnings Gap: A Review of Employment and Earnings Issues,* U.S. Department of Labor, Bureau of Labor Statistics, Report 673 (Government Printing Office, September 1982), table 4. The industry classifications used are two-digit SIC codes.

9. National Committee on Pay Equity and National Women's Political Caucus, *Who's Working for Working Women?* (Washington, D.C.: National Committee, 1984), p.1.

men and women assigned to them.[10] For example, although almost 58 percent of the employees of "eating and drinking places" are women, the number of employees who work in establishments that employ men or women exclusively or predominantly as waiters or waitresses is more than would be predicted by chance.[11]

Explaining the Differences

Wage differentials and segregation by occupation and industry might arise either from voluntary decisions untainted by discrimination or from choices forced upon women by discrimination—in the labor market or elsewhere. Many investigators have tried to measure the relative importance of each explanation. Some have done case studies or conducted interviews, and others have used statistical methods, typically regressing some measure of earnings on quantifiable factors thought to legitimately influence hourly wages and total earnings. The objective is to explain wage differences with such worker attributes as education, training, experience, health, hours worked, place of residence, and union membership.

CASE STUDIES

Several case studies indicate that people tend to favor men over women in otherwise identically defined situations. In one study, chairmen of academic departments were asked to review fictional files of candidates for faculty positions. The files came in pairs identical in all respects except the candidate's name. Men were 10 percent more likely to be regarded as deserving a tenured appointment. Another study, which applied the same methods to undergraduate business students who were screening applicants for managerial jobs, yielded similar results.[12] Female college students ranked paintings more favorably

10. William T. Bielby and James N. Baron, "A Woman's Place Is with Other Women: Sex Segregation within Organizations," in Barbara F. Reskin, ed., *Sex Segregation in the Workplace: Trends, Explanations, Remedies* (Washington, D.C: National Academy Press, 1984), p. 35.

11. Bureau of Labor Statistics, *Employment and Earnings,* vol. 32 (January 1985), p. 188. Segregation by establishment is examined by Francine D. Blau in *Equal Pay in the Office* (Lexington, Mass.: Lexington Books, 1977).

12. L. S. Fidell, "Empirical Verification of Sex Discrimination in Hiring Practices in Psychology," *American Psychologist,* vol. 25 (December 1970), pp. 1094–98; and Benson Rosen and Thomas H. Jerdee, "Effects of Applicant's Sex and Difficulty of Job

when informed they were the work of male artists than when they were described as being by female artists; when told a particular painting had won an award, the students indicated the sex of the artist did not matter.[13]

A Connecticut insurance company paid female raters $2,000 a year less than it paid male underwriters, although they did similar work. Another company hired male janitors to do heavy housekeeping (which meant pushing vacuum cleaners and waxing machines) and women to do light housekeeping (which meant washing and scrubbing by hand). In each of these cases, the male jobs were effectively closed to women, although the skills and requirements were similar.[14]

Another study reports how managers indicated they would handle specific management problems involving a given set of facts, one describing hypothetical cases involving women, one involving men.[15] Only the names were different. In general, the results indicated that the managers applied different standards to men and women. Women were more likely than men to be expected to attend the cocktail party thrown by the spouse's employer, to be granted leave for child care, and to be punished for tardiness, but they were less likely to be pressed to remain with the company if their spouse received an out-of-town job offer, to be apprised of management concern over an adulterous affair, to be sent to a training conference, or to be promoted.

STATISTICAL STUDIES

The standard statistical procedure for determining whether discrimination explains part of the male-female earnings gap is to try to relate pay differences to personal or job characteristics that most people acknowledge as legitimate influences on earnings, such as job tenure, years in the labor force, or education. If the average wage of men with given attributes is not significantly different from the average wage of women with equal attributes, discrimination is deemed not to occur.

---

on Evaluations of Candidates for Managerial Positions," *Journal of Applied Psychology*, vol. 59 (August 1974), pp. 511–12.

13. Gail I. Pheterson, Sara B. Kiesler, and Philip A. Goldberg, "Evaluation of the Performance of Women as a Function of Their Sex, Achievement, and Personal History," *Journal of Personality and Social Psychology*, vol. 19 (July 1971), pp. 114–18.

14. Sheila Tobias and Sharon Bernstein Medgal, "Rethinking Comparable Worth: Do All Roads Lead to Equity?" *Educational Record*, vol. 66 (Fall 1985), p. 30.

15. Benson Rosen and Thomas H. Jerdee, "Sex Stereotyping in the Executive Suite," *Harvard Business Review*, vol. 52 (March–April 1974), pp. 45–58.

These factors need not explain all variations in wages or earnings. Such unmeasured factors as luck and personality play a major part in everyone's economic fortunes, but there is no reason why luck or attractive personalities should be more prevalent among men than among women or should explain the male-female earnings gap.

Legitimate explanatory factors may not fully account for the earnings differential between men and women for two possible reasons. One is discrimination. The second is faulty analysis (or lack of data). Some legitimate factor may have been left out. The investigator may have made an error of statistical technique. Data may be lacking on some factor acknowledged to be important, a serious practical problem given the imperfection of surveys and the paucity of good case studies. In addition, it is always possible that some legitimate factor that is difficult or impossible to measure may be invoked as the real cause of any unexplained residual difference between male and female pay. For example, years of schooling might be similar for men and for women, but might conceal differences in curriculum that influence worker productivity.

Even if legitimate factors fully explain pay differences between men and women, discrimination is still possible. First, the legitimate factors themselves may be affected by discrimination. For example, past discrimination against women in admission to graduate professional schools may contribute to their current low earnings. Second, if women are better qualified than men on some variable omitted from the statistical analysis, then the fact that the included variables explain "only" the observed pay differences would suggest the presence of discrimination.

In short, no statistical exercise can ever prove definitively that any of the gap is caused by discrimination. Statistical studies are just one type of evidence that people should evaluate in deciding whether they think pay differences are attributable to discrimination.

Statistical studies have explained some, but not all, of the gap between male and female earnings. However, no study enumerated in a recent survey was able to explain more than half of the difference between male and female earnings without one or more explanatory variables designating the worker's occupation.[16] This legitimate deter-

16. Glen G. Cain, "The Economic Analysis of Labor Market Discrimination: A Survey," Special Report 37 (University of Wisconsin–Madison, Institute for Research on Poverty, March 1985), pp. 93–95. The gaps between male and female earnings

minant of earnings cannot be used to test for discrimination because discrimination is alleged to influence the occupations men and women choose.

Several patterns emerge from studies of male and female earnings.[17] First, the ratio of women's wages to men's is higher than the ratio of women's earnings or income to men's. The explanation is simple: women work fewer hours than men.

Second, the gap between women's and men's earnings increases with age. This pattern holds for both hourly and weekly wages. The widening of the earnings gap with age is consistent with the theory of human capital. According to that theory, people with strong commitments to the labor force invest more heavily in skills that increase their earnings later in their working lives than do people with little commitment to work. If women expect to withdraw from the labor force to bear and raise children, one would not expect them to invest as much in their future earnings capacity as men do, and their earnings would not grow as fast. Another and less sanguine interpretation of the age-graded decline in the female-male earnings ratio posits that women continue to be restricted to occupations with few opportunities for promotion, which would cause the female-male earnings gap to increase with age. The data do not clearly reject either explanation.

Third, the gap between hourly wages of women aged 20–24 and those of men the same age narrowed sharply in the early 1980s.[18] This fact is open to several interpretations. One may argue that young women today are more likely than in the past to have a commitment to lifelong involvement in the labor force and are moving into occupations that pay well or that have good opportunities for promotion. Or one may argue that discriminatory traditions are collapsing.

Fourth, taking years of experience into account increases substantially the proportion of the gap between male and female earnings that can be explained statistically.[19] This fact also is subject to conflicting

---

ranged from 15 percent to 68 percent, depending on the breadth or narrowness of the groups under consideration and the income variable under consideration.

17. Ibid., pp. 92–108.

18. James P. Smith and Michael P. Ward, *Women's Wages and Work in the Twentieth Century,* R-3119-NICHD (Santa Monica, Calif.: Rand Corp., 1984), pp. 22–25.

19. See research surveys by June A. O'Neill, reported in Equal Employment Advisory Council, *Comparable Worth: A Symposium on the Issues and Alternatives* (Washington, D.C.: EEAC, 1981), pp. 9–11; Cain, "Economic Analysis of Labor Market Discrimination," pp. 92–108.

interpretations. If women voluntarily quit jobs or leave the labor force more often than men do—for example, to move when their husbands change jobs or to have children—they will have less experience and earn lower pay than men do. On the other hand, women may leave the labor force more readily than men do because they are discouraged about the prospects of securing promotions or pay raises.[20]

Women's employment prospects could influence decisions about childbearing and child rearing; women with relatively poor prospects in the labor market might sense correctly that they sacrifice little by staying home to rear children. What appears to be a voluntary action—say, quitting a job—may be the rational accommodation to a discriminatory job market that offers little job security or opportunity for advancement. And what appears to be discriminatory behavior by employers may be their rational response to behavior that they cannot afford to ignore in hiring and promotion. In short, differences in earnings between men and women that are statistically related to work experience or family status may in some degree be explained by discrimination operating through these variables.

A fifth pattern revealed by statistical analyses of the differences in earnings between men and women is that the age-adjusted difference is smaller between women and men who have never married than it is between married women and men. Some argue that the differential between women and men who have never married is a better indicator of earnings differences because biologically and socially determined differences in child-rearing roles do not confuse the comparison. The problem with this interpretation is that men and women who remain single may do so for different reasons and have dissimilar characteristics. Never-married women earn more than women in general, while never-married men earn less than men in general.[21] The greater-than-average commitment to work of never-married women may offset other factors, possibly including discrimination, that explain the earnings gap.

Finally, much of the male-female wage gap is associated with job segregation among companies: that is, companies paying higher wages

20. See Stephen T. Marston, "Employment Instability and High Unemployment Rates," *Brookings Papers on Economic Activity, 1:1976*, pp. 179–83.

21. U.S. Bureau of the Census, *Current Population Reports*, series P-60, no. 142, "Money Income of Households, Families, and Persons in the United States: 1982" (GPO, 1984), table 45.

tend to hire men, and those paying lower wages tend to hire women. Thus eliminating wage differentials for workers with comparable education and training within companies would eliminate no more than one-tenth of the total wage gap.[22]

Lessons of Research

A survey of the statistical efforts to explain the gap between earnings of men and of women underscores an important lesson for legislators, judges, and others with responsibilities for passing or interpreting laws. That lesson is that statistical analyses of discrepancies between male and female earnings can neither confirm nor refute the hypothesis that women suffer from discrimination in the labor market. Such analyses can show that earnings or wage differentials are not fully explained by any number of measurable characteristics of men or women or the jobs they hold. But they cannot rule out the possibility that the discrepancy is caused by unmeasured variables other than discrimination and other than those included in the surveys on which these studies are based.[23] In particular, they cannot rule out the hypothesis that wage or earnings differences are the result of voluntary behavior.

Our own view is that labor market studies, not limited to statistical analyses of the causes of the male-female wage gap, support the commonsense notion that women have suffered extensive and damaging discrimination in the labor market. This view does not necessarily imply that comparable worth is the best remedy or even a constructive one. Nor does such a broad conclusion establish that in a particular case remediable discrimination has occurred. We shall turn to these issues below.

22. George Johnson and Gary Solon, "Pay Differences Between Women's and Men's Jobs: The Empirical Foundations of Comparable Worth Legislation," National Bureau of Economic Research Working Paper 1472 (Cambridge, Mass.: NBER, September 1984).

23. The range of explanatory variables used in statistical studies includes education, age, race, mental ability, formal training, labor market experience, marital status, health, tenure, size of city of residence, region of residence, socioeconomic status, quality of schooling, absenteeism record, turnover, occupation, class of worker, industry, union membership, type of employer, supervisory status, local labor market conditions, length of trip to work, and veteran status. However, not all of these variables have been used in any one study.

How Wages Are Set

The questions of whether the gap between male and female earnings can be narrowed by legal or administrative action without deleterious side effects and whether comparable worth will be more effective than other interventions depend on how labor markets work. Supporters and opponents of comparable worth disagree sharply on what underlies the typical wage-setting process. Paradoxically, however, there is no logical connection between the question of how labor markets operate and the issue of whether it is desirable to alter wages according to the principles of comparable worth. This section describes those conflicting views of labor markets.

The Standard Model

Adherents of the standard economic model tend to reject comparable worth as a rationale for closing the gap between male and female earnings. Their views rest on two propositions. First, if businesses produce output of given quality at minimum cost and if workers can choose among alternative jobs, wages will tend to equal the additional net revenue each worker generates for the employer. Employers would not pay workers less than their productivity because of fears that other employers would bid workers away by offering them wages commensurate with their productivity. Employers would not pay workers more than they contribute to net revenues because doing so would reduce net income and undermine the employer's power to compete. Thus wages should match productivity. Fulfillment of the condition that wages equal productivity over some time period requires either that managers can measure each worker's productivity or that they can grope toward such an understanding by trying various combinations of inputs, which would eventually reveal the best and cheapest methods of production. If all, or most, employers operate in this fashion, if workers have reasonably good information about job opportunities, and if certain other conditions are satisfied,[24] production will be economically efficient, in the sense that welfare is as high as it can be, given technology and workers' and consumers' preferences.

24. These conditions typically include the absence of monopoly and the collective provision of such goods as national defense or public health measures that private markets cannot be relied upon to provide.

The second proposition is that workers choose among jobs for which they qualify the one whose combination of wages and working conditions best satisfies them. If a worker is indifferent between two jobs, the job with inferior working conditions must offer higher pay just sufficient to compensate for nonwage disadvantages. Thus risky or unpleasant work is better paid than safe or pleasant work demanding comparable skills. The fact that some of the best-paid jobs are among the most pleasant and least risky does not refute this proposition, but merely reflects the high total compensation—pay plus working conditions—that people with valued skills or talents can command.

The validity of these two propositions guarantees that most workers will be employed in jobs where they are as productive as they can be, that they will be paid a wage that approximates their contribution to the company's net revenues, and that they will regard their total compensation—pay plus working conditions—as the best they can do.

These two propositions describe only tendencies. A shift in demand toward, say, computers will tend to raise the pay or lead to improved working conditions for computer programmers, relative to, say, nurses, although the training, education, intelligence, and energy required for each job is unaffected by the shift in demand. If wages for computer programmers stay high, new trainees can be expected to enter programming, and this inflow will reduce the wage differential. But wage differences unrelated to job or personal characteristics may persist for years. When workers with particular skills can find employment with only one or a few employers, the lack of good employment alternatives may prevent workers from getting wages their skills and productivity merit. In such cases, wages may remain below productivity indefinitely.

The first two propositions are sufficient but not necessary for a third: at higher wages, employers will demand fewer workers of a given type than they will demand at lower wages. This third proposition may hold even if the first two do not. If it is valid, then attempts to force up wages in particular occupations—for example, through comparable worth—will reduce employment in those occupations.

If all three propositions hold, nonmarket efforts to boost pay for particular occupations will reduce economic efficiency and employment in those occupations. Suppose, for example, that a job evaluation leads to higher wages for a particular worker or group of workers. If the new wage exceeds the market-validated wage, employers will lay off or fire workers, or not replace those who quit, until the productivity of those remaining at work matches the inflated wage. Those not employed will have to find work elsewhere in some job in which, presumably, the combination of pay and working conditions is inferior to those in the initial job (if they were better, the worker would have moved to the new job without other reasons). For example, a worker whose productivity is $10 per hour in job A and $9 per hour in job B would remain in job A if pay matched productivity and if working conditions were similar in both jobs. Some workers would be forced to move to job B if an increase to $11 in the job A wage led employers to curtail employment. Workers in job A who kept their jobs would gain, but those discharged or not hired because of the wage increase would lose, as would the owners of the business. Overall, output would fall because former job A workers would move into jobs where their productivity was reduced.

DISCRIMINATION

Labor market discrimination occurs when one group of workers is paid less than another for the same work, or when some workers are prevented from entering particular occupations, getting training, or winning promotion because of some characteristic irrelevant to job performance. The standard economic model is often linked to the view that labor market discrimination against any definable group is unlikely to persist. If any one company pays some workers less than they contribute to its net revenues, other companies have an incentive to try to bid such workers away from their current jobs. By offering such workers more than the artificially low pay they are receiving, other employers can get good workers inexpensively. The forces of competition, it is argued, will cause employers to undermine discrimination. Only if there is collusion or monopoly could one expect discrimination to persist. Segregation might survive indefinitely if one group of workers finds association with another distasteful. But so long as new companies, staffed by previously excluded, equally productive workers, are free to enter production, there is no reason, it is argued, for wage differences to continue.[25]

QUALIFICATIONS

Actual labor markets are far more complicated than this simplistic version of the standard model suggests. For example, a worker's contri-

25. The classic statement of this position is in Gary S. Becker, *The Economics of Discrimination,* 2d ed. (University of Chicago Press, 1971).

bution to a company's net revenues varies according to business conditions, but wage rates normally do not fully adjust to such short-run changes. Instead, workers typically receive constant salaries or wage rates for extended periods. The reconciliation of such wage or salary stability with variations in the value of output is a major preoccupation of current economic studies of the labor market.

In addition, the amount that a worker can contribute to a company's net revenues often depends on training or experience that cannot be easily transferred to other companies. As a result, employers and workers develop arrangements based on long-term commitments under which employers or employees invest in such training. In such cases, wages or earnings may not accurately reflect the worker's current contributions to the company's net revenues.

Complex and highly sophisticated theories have been developed to explain these long-term commitments within the theory of human capital. The human capital model rests on the view that employers pay workers their contribution to the company's net revenues over the long run, but it allows for significant deviations between wages and productivity lasting for many months or even years. It explains why employers incur costs to train their employees and why some forms of compensation—pensions, for example—are used to discourage employees from leaving a company even when it might be in their short-run interest to leave.[26]

Other Views of Labor Markets

Some economists, including both supporters and opponents of comparable worth, find unpersuasive the traditional view of how wages are set for most jobs. Employers would have to be able to accurately relate net revenue generated by individual workers to their activities. Skeptics question whether employers really know the productivity of workers in most jobs, even those involved with the production of physically measurable outputs sold at clearly defined prices. How much does a forklift operator who brings raw lumber to carpenters in a furniture mill add to the company's net revenues? How much does an elevator operator

26. Alan S. Blinder, "Private Pensions and Public Pensions: Theory and Fact," National Bureau of Economic Research Working Paper 902 (Cambridge, Mass.: NBER, June 1982).

working for a department store add to net revenues? How much does a librarian working in a university library add to the net revenues of the university? What about the driver of a municipal bus system, where the price of services may be set below cost as a matter of social policy? In the case of the university, the relationship between the activities of the librarian and revenue generation is virtually unfathomable. Tens of millions of jobs fall in the category where direct measurement of the value of output is arbitrary or impossible. Because government services are not marketed, their value is measured by cost. Many health services are reimbursed on the basis of cost. And, as noted, many jobs cannot be linked precisely to production.

In such cases, the wage is often determined not by any direct measurement of output on the current job, but by the prevailing scale for the particular job description and skill level. The responsible manager will pay the prevailing wage, and no more. At some point in the economy, it may be possible to identify a similar job, filled by people with similar attributes, where the value of output is directly measurable. But such connections may be remote and highly indirect, and in some cases—librarians, for example—there may be none.

In explaining how wages are set in such cases, critics of the traditional economic model emphasize the role of status, custom, convention, and habit. Wages, it is argued, are what they are—within a wide range—because workers and employers have come to accept them as fair and appropriate. Workers decide whether to go into particular jobs based on these understandings, and, unless a sharp change in the demand for particular skills occurs, wage patterns persist. But the persistence reflects the power of inertia and social acceptance, not the influence of productivity on compensation. Workers progress up job ladders, largely on a long-term basis inside individual companies or establishments, rather than by moving frequently among companies. These job ladders are relatively rigid, custom-bound sequences within which the connection between current wages and the productivity of current activities is loose or unknown.

If wages were modified through some external intervention, the argument runs, relative incomes would shift and the employment mix might change, as proposition three of the standard model would suggest. But in most cases there would be no reason to think that the allocation of labor had become less efficient, as propositions one and two would suggest. Lacking evidence that wages matched productivity to begin with, one would be hard pressed to prove that a change in relative wages moved them closer to or farther from such a match.

To the extent that this description of the loose or unprovable relationship between wages and productivity is valid, wage setting is heavily a social and political act, as well as an economic transaction. Wages become measures of power and social standing, as well as—or perhaps more than—signals of actual economic contributions.[27]

Another criticism of the traditional economic model supports the classic view that wages tend to match the contribution of workers to the company's net revenues, but holds that wages are set first and then jobs are shaped and workers trained so that the contributions of particular workers' jobs to the company's net revenues match the wages paid. From this perspective, wages are instruments for shaping the character of the labor force and the social relations that influence productivity in the workplace. However, in this view, as in the preceding one, it is difficult to predict the effect on productivity of any external intervention to change wages. If jobs have been shaped to match productivity to one wage structure, they could be shaped to fit another one, in which productivity could be either higher or lower.

The argument has been advanced that even if marginal productivity is measurable, competitive pressures may lead to dual labor markets, in which incumbents in some jobs have promotion opportunities and status while others do not.[28] This situation can arise if employers use above-normal wages to promote special job loyalty and effort. A contemporary description of conditions on Henry Ford's assembly lines claimed, "The Ford high wage does away with all of this inertia and . . . resistance. . . . The workmen are absolutely docile, and it is safe to say that, since the last day of 1912, every single day has seen marked reductions made in the Ford shops labor-costs."[29] Similarly, historian Allan Nevins reported:

27. Robert H. Frank suggests that wages may substitute for status in some jobs. His theory rationalizes the commonly observed tendency for some employers to promote workers by offering them more august titles and increased status as a substitute for increased pay. See Robert H. Frank, "Are Workers Paid Their Marginal Products?" *American Economic Review*, vol. 74 (September 1984), pp. 549–71.

28. Jeremy I. Bulow and Lawrence H. Summers, "A Theory of Dual Labor Markets with Application to Industrial Policy, Discrimination and Keynesian Unemployment," National Bureau of Economic Research Working Paper 1666 (Cambridge, Mass.: NBER, July 1985).

29. Horace Lucien Arnold and Fay Leone Faurote, *Ford Methods and the Ford Shops* (New York: Arno Press, 1972), p. 331.

> Ford and his associates freely declared on many occasions that the high wage policy had turned out to be good business. By this they meant that it had improved the discipline of the workers, given them a more loyal interest in the institution, and raised their personal efficiency. . . . Once the Ford factory, like others, had been called "The House of Correction"; now it was temporarily called "The House of Good Feeling."[30]

One of the traditional arguments for the optimality of the outcomes of competitive markets must clearly be rejected. The contention that ordinary labor markets tend to eliminate any form of systematic wage discrimination holds only under conditions that cannot be counted on to prevail. The desirable outcomes of all competitive markets hinge on the mutual possession of accurate information about exactly what is being bought and sold. Such information can reasonably be presumed for transactions in some kinds of commodities, but it cannot reasonably be assumed regarding purchases and sales of labor. Employers would have to know enough about the true productivity of employees to be able to ignore such external characteristics as race, sex, or age in hiring, training, and promotion. Furthermore, employers would have to be able to override any prejudices or preferences that current employees might hold regarding potential recruits. If they could not do so, they would have to be in a position to set up separate but equal workplaces to segregate the incompatible groups. The attitudes of current employees are important because they typically train and support new workers; if old employees are hostile, the transitional costs of bringing on new employees may be great enough to override any gains that might be achieved by eliminating previous discrimination-based inefficiencies.

In fact, employers lack good information about the actual productivity of prospective workers. All they can observe are external characteristics, supplemented in some cases by more or less accurate references from previous employers. And while employers can observe current employees, there is still some uncertainty about how they will respond to new incentives or training. As a result, employers may make hiring, training, or promotion decisions based on rules of thumb that limit opportunities for members of particular groups. Members of those groups, responding to the incentives they face, may behave in ways that ratify employers' rules of thumb. In such cases, externally imposed

30. Allan Nevins, *Ford: The Times, The Man, The Company* (Scribner, 1954), pp. 538, 549.

changes in rules—the prohibition of the use of sex, race, age, or other characteristics in hiring or promotion, or the use of affirmative action—may result in a larger output than would have occurred otherwise.[31]

Implications for Comparable Worth

Most opponents of comparable worth hold that labor markets work in a manner similar to that sketched by the standard model. Most supporters hold one of the alternative views of how labor markets work. Rather surprisingly, however, there is no logical connection between which theory most accurately characterizes labor markets and the desirability of adjusting wages according to the principles of comparable worth.

Even if one wholly accepts the traditional view of labor markets and rejects all of the criticisms, an important empirical question remains: will interfering with market-determined wages achieve other social objectives worth the sacrifice in efficiency? The trade-off between economic efficiency and distributional goals is pervasive and widely recognized.[32] People repeatedly elect officials who impose taxes and establish transfer programs that violate the conditions of economic efficiency to achieve some other purpose—to assist the needy, to sustain incomes of the elderly, or to promote institutions, such as museums or ballet companies, that free market forces seem inadequate to sustain.

31. The literature on the importance of information in the effective operation of competitive markets in general has been summarized elegantly in Joseph E. Stiglitz, "Information and Economic Analysis: A Perspective," *Economic Journal*, vol. 95 (1985, *Conference Papers*), pp. 21–41. The classic analyses of the importance of information in labor markets and of the possibility of persistent discrimination in the typical case when information is imperfect are A. Michael Spence, *Market Signaling: Informational Transfer in Hiring and Related Screening Processes* (Harvard University Press, 1974); Kenneth J. Arrow, "Models of Job Discrimination," in Anthony H. Pascal, ed., *Racial Discrimination in Economic Life* (Lexington, Mass.: Lexington Books, 1972), pp. 83–102; and George A. Akerlof, "The Market for 'Lemons': Quality Uncertainty and the Market Mechanism," *Quarterly Journal of Economics*, vol. 84 (August 1970), pp. 488–500. For a recent contribution demonstrating that discrimination is more likely to persist in small markets than in large ones, see George A. Akerlof, "Discriminatory, Status-based Wages among Tradition-oriented, Stochastically Trading Coconut Producers," *Journal of Political Economy*, vol. 93 (April 1985), pp. 265–76.

32. See Arthur M. Okun, *Equality and Efficiency: The Big Tradeoff* (Brookings, 1975).

However, even if one denies that labor markets generate economically efficient results, one might reject wage adjustments based on the principles of comparable worth. One might hold that some job loss is bound to result from pushing up wages in a particular occupation—a conclusion that would follow from an inverse relation between quantity demanded and price, but implies nothing about efficiency—and that the benefits from the wage gains for those who keep their jobs do not compensate for the losses suffered by those who lose theirs. Or one might argue that if comparable worth were implemented by the courts, those companies against which judgments happened to be brought first would be at a competitive disadvantage that would last until all competitors were also forced to adjust wages. Furthermore, and even more important, one might hold that better remedies are available for correcting the effects of discrimination against women or for raising their compensation—for example, steps to assure nondiscriminatory hiring and promotion, affirmative action to favor women, and special training programs to speed their advancement.

Theories about how labor markets work are relevant to the debate over comparable worth because they create expectations about the likely consequences of wage adjustments. According to the standard model, some loss of efficiency from such interference is unavoidable. According to the alternative views, no such loss of efficiency should be presumed. But theory cannot settle whether the gains from wage adjustments justify any loss of efficiency or whether there are better instruments for improving the position of women in the labor market.

Job Evaluation

Setting wages according to the principles of comparable worth requires some form of direct job evaluation. Some appreciation of how wage setting has evolved in the United States is essential for understanding the place of job evaluation. Until the late nineteenth century workers in many industries were hired, managed, paid, and fired at the sole discretion of shop foremen.[33] A plant might employ many fore-

33. For descriptions of this process, see Sanford M. Jacoby, "The Development of Internal Labor Markets in American Manufacturing Firms," and Bernard Elbaum, "The Making and Shaping of Job and Pay Structures in the Iron and Steel Industry," in Paul Osterman, ed., *Internal Labor Markets* (MIT Press, 1984), pp. 23–107.

men. Unemployment was high enough in most years to permit foremen considerable latitude in exercising their power.

> In most firms the foreman was given free rein to manage the acquisition, payment, and supervision of labor. . . . The foreman's control over employment began literally at factory gates. On mornings when the firm was hiring—a fact advertised by newspaper ads, signs, or word of mouth—a crowd gathered in front of the factory. The foreman stood at the head of the crowd and picked out those workers who appeared suitable or had managed to get near front. . . . Assignment to a job was determined in large part by favoritism or prejudice. . . . The foreman also had considerable power to determine the wages of the workers he hired. . . . Variations in rates across departments were common because each foreman ran his shop autonomously. Employment and wage records were rarely kept before 1900; only the foreman knew with any accuracy how many workers were employed in his department and the rates they received. Foremen jealously guarded wage information, allowing them to play favorites by varying the day rate or assigning favored workers to jobs where piece rates were loose.[34]

The Emergence of Job Evaluation

Gradually middle management and personnel departments assumed the powers once exercised by foremen. The prosperity of the World War I era and the 1920s spurred the advance of unionism and the interest of management in regularizing working conditions. As unemployment dropped, the power of foremen to exercise discipline and to use the threat of discharge to elicit maximum effort began to wane; something other than raw power was needed to maintain worker effort. Large companies introduced personnel departments during World War I and thereafter. At first, these departments lacked broad power, but they acquired it gradually over a period of decades. Only in the years following World War II did personnel departments acquire substantial power over rules governing hiring, wage setting, promotion, and dismissal.

Job evaluation has had a similar history, but has lagged behind the assumption of responsibility for wage setting by management. Job evaluation was first used over one hundred years ago by the U.S. Civil Service Commission, but it was not employed widely in the private sector until World War II. The National War Labor Board's policy of granting wage increases only for the purpose of correcting demon-

34. Jacoby, "The Development of Internal Labor Markets," pp. 25–26.

strated inequities encouraged the use of job evaluation. At about the same time, government jobs became subject to classification under some form of job evaluation. The federal government's General Schedule (GS) system was the most notable. The use of job evaluation is now widespread, but the number of workers covered is unknown.[35]

Job evaluation deals with jobs, not their incumbents. It provides an estimate of the value of a job to a company based on the tasks, responsibilities, and conditions associated with the job. Who fills the job or what that person is paid has nothing directly to do with the evaluation of the job. Thus the evaluation of a particular sales job is the same whether the job happens to be filled by a high school dropout or a Ph.D. physicist. Managers have the responsibility to use information on education, training, experience, and other characteristics to match people to work for which they are best suited.

A variety of job evaluation formulas exists.[36] All involve the identification of a number of job attributes, the scaling or measurement of the amounts of each attribute required for a particular job, and the assignment of weights or values to that attribute.

The number of factors used in job evaluation systems typically ranges from four to twelve or more. The number differs in part because evaluation systems were first developed for different kinds of work—office jobs, production jobs, executive jobs, or special occupations—and in part because judgments differ about the importance of various job attributes. The Midwest Industrial Management Association job evaluation plan, for example, lists eleven attributes for shop jobs and eleven for office jobs. Some attributes are on both lists—education and experience, for example—but most are on only one. Shop jobs entail such attributes as "initiative and ingenuity," "physical demand," "responsibility for equipment," and "hazardous working conditions." Office jobs entail such attributes as "complexity of duties," "effect of errors," "contact with others," "working conditions," and "type and extent of supervision of others." The federal government uses nine factors in classifying jobs for its general schedule. The state of Idaho uses eight. Private consulting companies have developed similar evaluation systems for use in either the private or public sectors.

35. Donald J. Treiman, *Job Evaluation: An Analytic Review* (Washington, D.C.: National Academy of Sciences, 1979), p. 1.

36. The following description is based largely on information contained in ibid., chap. 2.

In most systems, each job is assigned a certain number of points chosen from a scale for each attribute in the job evaluation system. For example, the number of points allowed under the federal government's general schedule for "knowledge required by the position" ranges from 50 points for the most menial jobs to 1,850 for the most advanced. The number of points for "supervisory controls" ranges from 25 for the least independent jobs to 650 for senior supervisors. The points for all job attributes are added, and the resulting score measures the value of the job. Jobs are then ranked according to point scores, which serve as the basis for determining the pay for each job.

This history and description of job evaluation underscore that it traditionally has been used to remove anomalies from wage structures otherwise found to be acceptable, not to change the wage structures in fundamental ways. The objective has been to align wages for particular jobs with wages paid for other jobs with similar characteristics. Thus a given employer might use different job evaluation systems for office and production workers and typically will make no attempt to compare any office job with any production job even if jobs in the two sectors happen to be quite similar. The implicit assumption in traditional job evaluation has been that differences in characteristics among workers performing jobs with similar attributes were too small to matter in setting wages. This approach to job evaluation has been christened "policy capturing."

Ordinary job evaluation is seldom applied rigidly. Job evaluation consultants rely on market forces when identifying factors and setting weights for job evaluation. Market wages may also be used to modify the results of the job evaluation process itself. Where the conflict is sharp between prevailing wages and what a job evaluation says a job is worth, employers defer to the market. One result is that although two jobs may score similarly in job evaluations—nurses and computer programmers, for example—market forces may cause one job—nurses—to be paid less than its evaluation would suggest, and another—programmers—to be paid more.

Comparable worth advocates employ job evaluation differently. They would use it to alter the wage structure in fundamental ways for the benefit of particular groups of workers. Job evaluation is often used to justify the payment of wages higher than employers have found adequate to attract employees. Jobs held by men are used to determine how much particular job attributes are worth. These values are then used to impute a wage to jobs held predominantly by women. In effect, this use of job evaluation accepts the current structure of wages for jobs filled by men (in other words, it is "policy capturing"), but not for jobs held predominantly by women. Put another way, it requires that job characteristics be valued the same regardless of which sex usually fills the job.

Critique of Job Evaluation

Despite the apparent formality and objectivity of job evaluation, the procedures are judgmental throughout. In no sense do they represent an objective determination of the value of the marginal product of each job. Subjective evaluations enter at every step of the way: in determining what attributes to include in the job evaluation, in setting the point weights for each attribute, in deciding how many points each job should get for each attribute, and in calibrating the resulting point scores with pay.[37]

An example is the range of weights attached to the degree of supervision required in an office job: one job evaluation scale assigns a maximum of 7 percent of total points to this attribute while another assigns 14.5 percent. "Physical demand" provides a maximum of 10 percent of the points for one evaluation plan for shop jobs, but none at all for office jobs. Some job evaluation scales are meant to apply only to shop jobs, others only to office jobs, and still others to both.[38]

The importance of a particular attribute in determining a job's rank depends not on the *maximum* proportion of total points it could account for, but on the *proportion* of the variation in total points of the various jobs it actually accounts for. Actual variation depends purely on the judgment of evaluators.[39]

In practice, jobs rank differently according to various job evaluation scales. How job attributes are weighted can determine how jobs are

37. Leslie Zebrowitz McArthur stresses the prominence of value judgments in job evaluations in "Social Judgment Biases in Comparable Worth Analysis," in Hartmann, ed., *Comparable Worth*, pp. 53–70.

38. Treiman, *Job Evaluation*, pp. 66–170.

39. Suppose, for example, that jobs are ranked entirely on the basis of two factors, "brain" and "brawn." Jobs are assigned from 0 to 100 points for "brains" and from 0 to 30 points for "brawn." Brains appears to be the more important factor, because it can account for 100 out of 130 maximum points. Suppose, however, that most jobs are assigned similar "brains" scores (say, most jobs are clustered in a 10-point range from

ranked.[40] In fact, different relative rankings of different jobs may arise for any of a variety of reasons: use of different attributes or different weights or differences in the application of a given system by different evaluators. The simple correlations between the rankings of various evaluators applying the same job evaluation system are sometimes disturbingly low.[41]

Use of Job Evaluations in Comparable Worth Disputes

Job evaluations might be used in a variety of ways in disputes over pay equity. First, they might be used to help determine whether differences among job characteristics suffice to explain why women are paid less than men. A finding that job characteristics do not explain wage differentials, together with other evidence, can support a claim that legally remediable wage discrimination exists. Whether one thinks that wage adjustments should be triggered by the mere showing of such an unexplained wage gap or that adjustments should hinge on additional evidence that the wage gap results from discriminatory behavior, in either case job evaluations would need only to show broad differences between the compensation of men and women performing similarly evaluated jobs. There would be no need for different evaluations to yield the same ranking of any particular pair of jobs. Results that were less than perfectly consistent would suffice.

Second, job evaluation might be used, after a finding that compensation is illegally discriminatory, to set new wages. Whatever the basis for such a finding, the requirements for consistency among alternative methods of job evaluation would be stringent. Setting new wages by job evaluations that ranked pairs of jobs differently would be impossible

---

40 to 50 points), but the scores are widely distributed over the 30-point range for "brawn." In that event, brawn will be more important than brains in determining the rankings.

40. Suppose jobs are ranked according to two factors, A and B, and are given scores for each factor ranging from 1 to 10. Job I is given a score of 3 for factor A and 8 for factor B. Job II is given a score of 5 for factor A and 7 for factor B. If each factor is weighted equally, job II ranks ahead of job I (12 points to 11). If factor B is accorded, say, three times the weight of factor A, however, job I will rank head of job II (27 points to 26).

41. Donald P. Schwab documents that the correlation among job evaluations ranges widely. In some cases the rankings were almost identical, while in other cases the correlation was well below 0.5. "Job Evaluation Research and Research Needs," in Hartmann, ed., *Comparable Worth*, pp. 37–52.

unless there were some rational basis for preferring one evaluation over another.

We hold that job evaluations, if done with care, could be used for the first of these purposes—that is, to analyze the sources of pay gaps between men and women—but that they are not sufficiently accurate or reliable to be used for the second purpose—to set new wage scales after a finding of discrimination. The following example illustrates the reasons for this position. It is based on actual wages and job evaluation scores assigned to 117 government jobs in the state of Washington.[42]

A simple way to relate the wage actually paid to incumbents of job i, w_i, to the point score for job i, p_i, is:

$$w_i = a + b\,p_i + c\,D, \tag{1}$$

where

a = a constant term;
b = the number of dollars of wage per point in the job evaluation;
c = the wage difference between men's and women's jobs not explained by job evaluation points;
D = 0 for jobs filled predominantly by men and 1 for jobs filled predominantly by women.

A finding that the coefficient, c, is significantly less than zero would mean that women are paid less than men in jobs judged similar according to the criteria used in the job evaluation. This approach makes sense if one believes that the wage structure for men's jobs basically makes sense but that there may be anomalies—jobs whose actual pay does not correspond to the productivity that job evaluation allegedly measures correctly. Alternatively, if one believes that the wage structure exhibits no particular relation to productivity, b could be selected on the basis of individual judgments, collective bargaining, or other techniques. A slight variation of equation 1 would replace variable D with one measuring the proportion of the incumbents of each job who are women.

Fitting wages to job points would produce a relation like that shown in figure 1, which is based on actual data from the state government of Washington. There is no reason, however, why the mathematical form

42. Norman D. Willis, *State of Washington Comparable Worth Study* (Seattle: Norman D. Willis and Associates, 1974).

Figure 1. *Relation of Salary to Job Points, by Sex*[a]

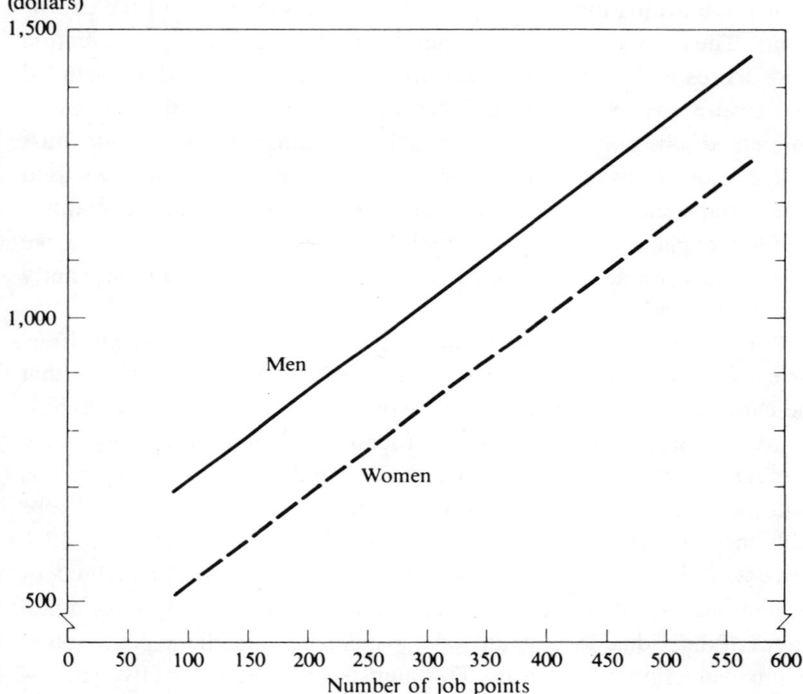

a. Derived from appendix equation A-1.

in equation 1 should be employed or have any particular appeal. Any number of alternative mathematical forms could be employed for translating job evaluation point scores into wages. Equations 2 through 5, which omit the variable showing the sex of employees, list four such alternatives; many others would be equally appealing.

$$w_i = a + b\,p_i - g\,p_i^2; \quad (2)$$

$$w_i = a + b \log p_i; \quad (3)$$

$$w_i = c(p_i)^b; \quad (4)$$

$$\log w_i = a + b\,p_i. \quad (5)$$

Equation 2 differs from equation 1 in that it includes not only job points but also job points squared, where g is the coefficient. Equations 3–5 represent other mathematical transformations of the relation between wages and job points. In each case, actual wages could be regressed against job evaluation point scores to estimate the values of the coefficients. These coefficients could then be used to translate job evaluation point scores into wages. As in equation 1, a variable could be included to measure any systematic differences between wages paid in male-dominated jobs and those paid in female-dominated jobs. In our illustrative calculations based on data from the state of Washington, we used four variants each of equations 1 through 5. The Appendix contains a detailed explanation of our statistical procedures. In each case we included a variable to indicate whether a job was filled predominantly by men or by women.

For purposes of suggesting the existence of sex-based wage differences, it is sufficient to find that the coefficient of the variable that indicates a job is filled mostly by women is consistently and significantly negative. That is what we found. For jobs with the average number of job points, women are paid from 22.2 to 27.2 percent less than men are paid, depending on the method of estimation.[43] For jobs with the highest number of job points, women are paid from 12.6 percent to 23.9 percent less than men, depending on the method of estimation. We then used these equations to calculate by how much wages of individual jobs would have to change to match the pay implied by job evaluation point scores. This adjustment consisted of two parts—changes, up or down, based upon job point scores, and additional changes to remove the consistent shortfall of pay for women's jobs relative to that for men's.

The results of this exercise are displayed in figures 2 and 3. These figures show that incumbents of jobs filled predominantly by women in the state of Washington typically receive lower salaries relative to job evaluation point scores than do incumbents of jobs filled predominantly by men.[44]

43. The comparison is the range of estimates generated by the equations shown in the Appendix.

44. This pattern holds on the average, but not in every case. Mental health specialists, 89 percent of whom are men, would receive among the largest pay increases. Some equations in the Willis study suggest that three jobs filled predominantly by women—librarian-level III, nursing care consultant, and school food services supervisor—might have their pay cut (Willis, *Comparable Worth Study,* p. 10). But, on balance, application of these job evaluation data would clearly lead to an increase in women's pay. It is statistically possible for pay differences associated with the workers' sex to vary not only

Figure 2. *Range of Differences between Predicted and Current Men's Wages*[a]

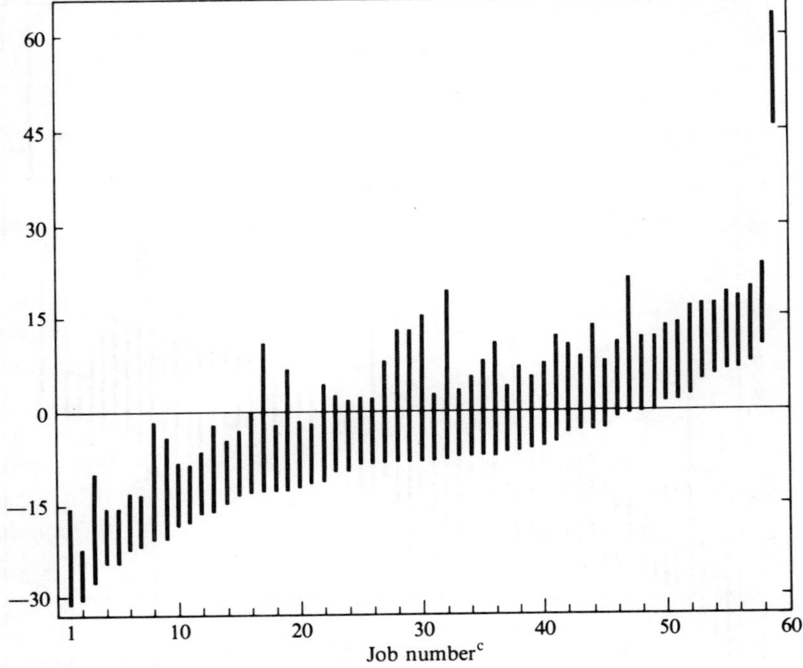

a. Estimated from appendix equations A-1 through A-20.

b. The range of percentage changes from each job's current wage to the wages estimated from the twenty equations.

c. Arrayed in order by the minimum change estimated from any of the equations.

But these results also reveal that equally defensible statistical analyses of job evaluation data can yield widely varying estimates of the amounts by which wages on particular jobs should be changed. For

---

with the mathematical form of the equation used to relate wages to job points, but also with the weighting scheme used to construct job points. Thus increasing the relative importance given to low-scoring job attributes of jobs filled primarily by women could eliminate the result, shown in figures 2 and 3, that men are paid more than women for jobs with similar job point scores. We were unable to test this possibility because the job evaluation data for Washington State included only the final point scores, not the number of points assigned for each job attribute. According to Helen Remick of the University of Washington, reweighting would be unlikely to have much effect on the relative ranking of jobs because the correlation among the scores on each pair of the attributes exceeded 0.9.

Figure 3. *Range of Differences between Predicted and Current Women's Wages*[a]

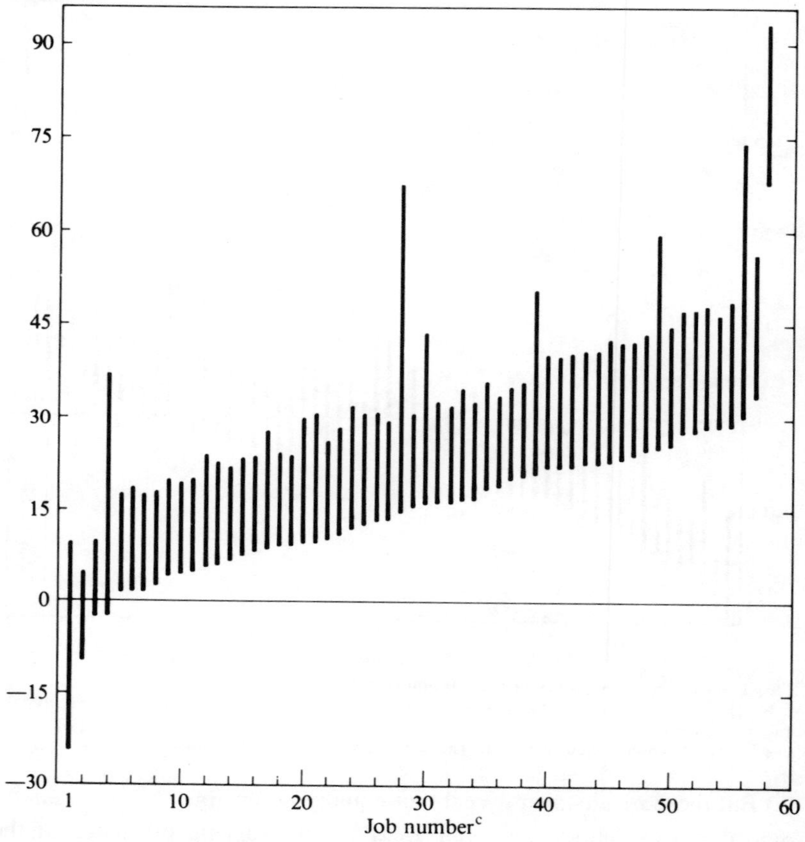

a. Estimated from appendix equations A-1 through A-20.

b. The range of percentage changes from each job's current wage to the wages estimated from the twenty equations.

c. Arrayed in order by the minimum change estimated from any of the equations.

some jobs, it is not even clear whether wages should be increased or decreased. Table 3 lists eight occupations for which some equations indicate that wages should be cut, while other equations indicate that wages should be increased; in all of these cases, the range from the highest to the lowest estimated wage is at least 20 percent of the original wage. Table 3 also lists two other jobs for which the spread between the

Table 3. *Changes in Estimated Wages as a Result of Alternative Equations*[a]
Percent

Occupation	*Estimated wage change*	
	Minimum	*Maximum*
Predominantly female jobs		
Unemployment insurance actuary	−2.3	37.3
School food services supervisor	−24.1	9.7
Registered nurse IV	14.5	67.7
Administrative services manager A	30.2	74.2
Predominantly male jobs		
Highway maintenance superintendent	−8.0	19.4
Driver mail carrier	−8.4	15.3
Custodian II	−0.8	21.6
Animal technician II	−8.4	12.7
Utilities maintenance worker	−8.4	12.7
Traffic guide	−12.7	10.9

Source: Authors' estimates based on equations A-1 through A-20.
a. See equations 1–5 and discussion in text.

wage corrections implied by the various equations was more than 40 percent.

This analysis suggests that *if* one believes in job evaluation techniques, then wages for jobs filled by women are lower in Washington than are wages for comparable jobs filled by men. It is possible that discrimination influenced which jobs men or women chose and that personal rather than job characteristics explain wage differences. Even if one strongly believes in job evaluation, however, such results cannot establish the proper wage for particular jobs. Nor do these calculations indicate how estimates of the male-female wage gap in these jobs would be modified by adding other variables, such as age, education, or work experience.

Sharon Smith has argued forcefully that it is absurd to use job evaluation rigidly to rank jobs.[45] She describes a hypothetical situation in which wages are being set for Spanish-English and French-English translators. According to the criteria of job evaluation, these two occupations surely would be ranked similarly, as the educational requirements, experience, working conditions, and other characteristics of each job are similar. By the criteria of job evaluation, people perform-

45. Cited in Michael Evan Gold, *A Dialogue on Comparable Worth* (Ithaca, N.Y.: Industrial and Labor Relations Press, 1983), pp. 43–44.

ing these two jobs should be paid similar wages. But, Smith asks, would one expect wages to be similar in, say, Miami? The supply of people fluent in Spanish is certainly higher there, but the demand for Spanish translators may also be higher. Spanish translators might end up being paid either more or less than French translators, but there is no good reason to argue that the wages should be identical. Smith uses this example to support her contention that attempts to determine the intrinsic value of a job to an employer are futile; the wage that an employer will pay depends on how many workers are available at what wage (supply) and how much value is placed on the worker's services (demand).[46]

Despite these qualifications, job evaluation has long played an important part in the determination of wages in many industries. There is every prospect that it will continue to do so. The results of job evaluation are relevant to, although not decisive in, disputes over whether the pay gap between men and women can be fully explained by factors other than discrimination.

What Comparable Worth Entails

Studies of comparable worth, in the guise of job evaluation, have been around for a long time, and many private businesses and government entities have been using job evaluation both to establish which jobs are comparable and hence should be paid the same and to identify differences among jobs that could be used for establishing pay scales. So what would be new about applying job evaluation to the male-female wage gap? The answer is that to use job evaluation to bring order out of a chaotic wage structure is one thing; to use it to fundamentally change the wage structure is something altogether different. Quite apart from the question of whether this new use for job evaluation would be desirable, there is the practical question of whether it would

46. Even if the world functioned strictly according to neoclassical economic principles, with short adjustment periods, this telling example is open to some qualification. If extraordinary excess supply led to lower wages for, say, Spanish translators than for French translators, employers might respond by asking Spanish translators to perform more menial tasks than those customarily required of translators. For example, they might be provided less advanced equipment or less secretarial assistance. The point is that the lower wage for Spanish translators would cause a typical employer to spend less on, say, equipment to economize on their time or to change the job they were asked to do. After an adjustment period, the jobs of Spanish translator and French translator would cease to be the same.

be administratively feasible. Would it strengthen labor markets (as its proponents claim), destroy the foundations of the U.S. economic system (as its opponents assert), or perhaps have less dramatic or less certain effects than either supporters or opponents allege? Is it the most effective way to deal with sex-based discrimination in the labor market?

The State and Local Level

Proponents hold that public and nonprofit employers should carry out comparable worth studies similar to those carried out in the state of Washington and being implemented in several other jurisdictions. They point to the wage adjustments, based on comparable worth studies, by the city of San José, the state of Minnesota, and several other governments.

In July 1981 the city of San José agreed to pay its employees represented by the American Federation of State, County, and Municipal Employees $1.45 million over two years as comparable worth pay adjustments. The settlement was reached after a nine-day strike, which erupted when lengthy negotiations failed to produce an agreement on comparable worth pay adjustments and cost-of-living increases in the 1981 contract. The union's claims for comparable worth adjustments were based on the results of a December 1980 study by Hay Associates that revealed female-dominated jobs to be underpaid relative to male-dominated jobs of equal value. Actual payments totaled $6.8 million over five years, rising from $585,000 in fiscal year 1981 to $1.9 million in fiscal 1985.[47]

During its 1982 session, the Minnesota legislature passed comparable worth legislation affecting 9,000 state employees. The legislation was passed after job evaluation studies revealed that the average salary differential between male- and female-dominated jobs, felt to be mainly a product of job segregation, was about 25 percent. In light of these findings, the legislature passed a law that called for a job evaluation study of positions in the civil service system every two years. If undercompensation was found to exist, the law mandated that salary increases be negotiated through collective bargaining. The state appropriated $21.8 million for pay equity adjustments during 1983–84. It claims to have eliminated about half of the discrepancy between wages

47. Janet A. Flammang, "Effective Implementation: The Case of Comparable Worth in San José," paper prepared for the 1984 annual meeting of the Association for Public Policy Analysis and Management, app. B.

and job values as determined by the evaluation study. The state's job classification system was studied again in 1985, when findings of salary inequities were presented to the legislature for pay equity adjustment appropriations.

In 1984 Minnesota broadened its comparable worth policy by requiring municipalities to provide equal pay for work of comparable value. This statute applies to approximately 150,000 workers employed by cities, townships, utilities, districts, and counties.[48]

Between 1977 and September 1983 twenty-six states had enacted or adopted laws or resolutions on comparable worth. These measures prohibit employers from discriminating between the sexes in the payment of wages or employing a female at a salary or wage less than that paid to a male employee for work of *comparable* character. During 1982 and 1983 legislatures in California, Iowa, Minnesota, Montana, Oregon, and Washington enacted measures seeking to establish statewide standards of equal pay for work of comparable value, and Nevada and Massachusetts began studies of comparable worth in state employment. New York, New Jersey, and Maryland have established task forces to study pay equity in state employment. Virginia and Rhode Island have adopted legislative resolutions for such studies, while Kentucky, Maine, and Wisconsin have enacted stricter measures to enforce pay equity provisions.

Other states have moved beyond study to implementation of the results of pay equity reports. New Mexico appropriated $3.3 million in 1983 to increase the salaries of the state's lowest-paying jobs. Iowa began a $10 million comparable worth plan for 1984–85 in 1984, and hopes to achieve comparability by 1987. The Connecticut legislature has approved and funded three separate and successive steps to undertake and implement the results of pay equity studies; the culmination will be an evaluation of every job title in the state's classification system.[49]

Public Sector and Private Sector

There are several reasons for emphasizing public-sector jobs. Disproportionately, that is where women work; in 1984 women filled 51

48. *Wall Street Journal*, May 10, 1985; and Bureau of National Affairs, *Pay Equity and Comparable Worth* (Washington, D.C.: BNA, 1984), pp. 58–59.

49. National Committee on Pay Equity, *Who's Working*, pp. 33–35; Bureau of National Affairs, *Pay Equity and Comparable Worth*, p. 56; and authors' telephone interviews.

percent of public-sector jobs versus 43.5 percent of private-sector jobs.[50] In addition, public-sector workers are being unionized by one of the few major unions that has recruited successfully during the 1970s and 1980s, the American Federation of State, County, and Municipal Employees. The allegation of wage discrimination, together with the promise that discrimination can be corrected, is a powerful organizing tool.[51] An analytical reason for emphasizing the public sector is that the market cannot accurately measure the value of the marginal product of workers who produce most government goods and services, because they are not marketed. Although many public-sector jobs have private-market counterparts, where productivity can sometimes be measured and where wages sometimes can be set objectively, the public sector so dominates some occupations and labor markets that it effectively determines wages in them.

Supporters of comparable worth would encourage the use of job evaluation in the private sector as well, but would require employers who carry out such evaluations to act on the results. If employers fail to do so, advocates argue that aggrieved workers should have legal recourse to compel enforcement through administrative proceedings or in the courts.

Precisely what "implementing the results of job evaluations" means is not clear. In the Equal Pay Act of 1963, Congress prohibited unequal pay for *equal* work and stipulated that where unequal pay was proven, reductions in compensation of the higher-paid workers were prohibited and the compensation of workers with lower pay had to be increased.[52]

50. Bureau of Labor Statistics, *Employment and Earnings*, vol. 32 (January 1985), p. 181.

51. The American Federation of State, County, and Municipal Employees "has used pay equity as an effective organizing tool. In two recent close elections involving 3,000 and 7,500 eligible voters, AFSCME successfully made its approach to pay equity a major campaign issue, winning each election by 80–85 votes." Winn Newman, "Pay Equity: A Union Perspective," testimony presented to New York State Chamber of Commerce and Industry, March 11, 1982.

52. "No employer having employees subject to any provisions of this section shall discriminate . . . between employees on the basis of sex by paying wages to employees . . . at a rate less than the rate at which he pays wages to employees of the opposite sex . . . for equal work . . . which requires equal skill, effort, and responsibility, and which [is] performed under similar working conditions, except where such payment is made pursuant to (i) a seniority system; (ii) a merit system; (iii) a system which measures earnings by quantity or quality of production; or (iv) a differential based on any other factor other than sex: *Provided*, That an employer who is paying a wage rate differential in violation of this subsection shall not, in order to comply with the provisions of this subsection, reduce the wage rate of any employee." Equal Pay Act of 1963, 29 U.S.C. 206(d) (1975).

If this principle were extended to require wage increases for workers found to be getting less pay than other workers for *comparable* work, far more workers would be affected. Courts would have to decide whether wage reductions as well as wage increases would be allowable where comparable—rather than identical—work was involved. They would also have to choose among contending job evaluations and determine the period over which corrections could be made. To the extent that comparable worth is applied to private-sector workers, comparable worth supporters agree that wage comparisons should be made only within establishments, or within companies when wage scales span all the establishments of a single company. They oppose trying to establish wage norms within or across industries.

The Australian Experience

The only example of the consequences that would result from widespread application of comparable worth comes from Australia, where women's wages were increased substantially and quickly to establish the principle of equal pay for comparable worth. Wages are set and grievances are resolved through a complex system of administrative commissions and quasi-judicial proceedings.[53] The national authorities adopted the principle of "equal pay for equal work" in 1969. A second decision in 1972, to be implemented in stages by mid-1975, called for "equal pay for work of equal value." As a result of these decisions, base pay for women, as determined by Australia's centralized wage-setting Conciliation and Arbitration Commission, rose from 74 percent of that of men in 1970 to 94 percent by the end of the decade. The ratio of women's to men's earnings rose from 65 percent to 86 percent. These changes in relative wages cannot be traced to changes in occupational structure or other economic factors.

The consequences of this sharp wage adjustment remain in dispute. After examining the Australian experience, Daniel Mitchell concluded:

> Economists are prone to believe that significant changes in relative prices or wages will lead to important changes in resource allocation, and they have struggled to find symptoms of such effects after the equal pay decisions. Yet the gross numbers show that the proportion of women in

53. For a detailed description of the wage-setting process, see Daniel J. B. Mitchell, "The Australian Labor Market," in Richard E. Caves and Lawrence B. Krause, eds., *The Australian Economy: A View from the North* (Brookings, 1984), pp. 127–93.

Australia's labor force and in total employment kept rising in the late 1970s, and that the ratio between unemployment rates for women and those for men did not rise (it fell). Researchers have had to "tease" the data to come up with any signs that the demand for women relative to men was reduced.[54]

In contrast, Robert Gregory and Robert Duncan estimated that the Australian experiment with pay equalization had a perceptible impact on the growth of female employment and on the female unemployment rate.[55] They report estimates that pay equalization slowed growth of women's employment by one-third, led to fewer hours worked per week, and increased women's unemployment by about 0.5 percentage point. Despite these findings, Gregory and Duncan also expressed surprise that the large changes in relative pay of men and women had such modest effects on labor demand.

An Agenda

In deciding whether and how wage adjustments based on comparable worth should be used in settling claims of wage discrimination against women, one must take a stand on four questions. First, how serious is the problem of wage discrimination against women? Second, will wage adjustments based on comparable worth contribute to a solution of the problem? Third, what side effects will the intervention produce? Fourth, are there other instruments available for dealing with the problem that will be more effective or produce fewer side effects?

On the first question, we have shown that the facts on wage discrimination against women are in dispute. No one questions that women are

54. Ibid., p. 134. Mitchell goes on to note that the ratio of women employees to total employees, which rose 1.9 percent per year from 1966 to 1970, grew more slowly thereafter. As a result, women constituted only 36.7 percent of all employees by 1982, instead of the 40 percent that would have resulted had the growth rates of the late 1960s been maintained. Mitchell suggests that part of this slowdown may have been attributable to the changes in relative pay, but then concludes, "Whatever the reasons for the slowdown in Australia, economists no doubt were surprised (disappointed?) that it was not larger."

55. Robert G. Gregory and Robert C. Duncan, "Segmented Labor Market Theories and the Australian Experience of Equal Pay for Women," *Journal of Post Keynesian Economics,* vol. 3 (Spring 1981), pp. 403–28. For a summary of their findings, see Mark R. Killingsworth, "The Economics of Comparable Worth: Analytical, Empirical, and Policy Questions," in Hartmann, ed., *Comparable Worth,* pp. 105–07.

paid less than men. However, the contribution of various influences to this gap is unclear. Part of the wage gap reflects social roles for whose effects the courts cannot compensate. Part reflects discriminatory behavior clearly prohibited by federal legislation. We suggest that the preponderance of evidence shows some of the gap also arises from lower compensation for jobs filled primarily by women than for similar jobs performed by men.

Wage adjustments based on comparable worth can reduce the wage gap within particular firms. But much of the gap is attributable to the fact that companies with mostly male employees tend to pay higher wages than do companies with mostly female employees (see table 2). This fact means that elimination of the wage gap between men and women will require measures other than wage adjustments based on comparable worth.

Evidence on whether the wage structure compensates workers according to their productivity, a necessary condition for economic efficiency, is conflicting. The effects of imposed changes in the wage structure on economic efficiency are therefore also uncertain.

Our judgment on the first two questions is that the relatively low pay of women is a serious problem, but that only a small part of that low pay can be remedied by wage adjustment based on comparable worth. Furthermore, wage adjustment based on comparable worth is only one of a number of possible ways of correcting for labor market discrimination. Against this background, we suggest that neither wholehearted embrace nor unambiguous rejection of wage adjustments by the courts or legislatures is warranted. Rather, this situation is one in which the best course is legislative and judicial imprecision, an environment within which the courts can engage in a protracted process of fact finding and consensus building.

Unions

Unless prohibited by law, union organizers will continue to court new members with promises to seek pay equity based on comparable worth through negotiation, much as they have long been using the promise to seek fair wages through negotiation and collective bargaining, work stoppages, or other techniques.[56] For example, unions have

56. The AFL-CIO unanimously adopted a comparable worth policy at its 1985 convention. The AFL-CIO denies that any of its members are opposed to comparable worth as policy, but acknowledges that some local unions have quarreled with the

contributed to a significant narrowing of differences in wages within certain occupations.[57] The degree to which they succeed in causing employers to realign wages in traditionally male or female jobs would depend in the future, as it has in the past, on their ability to mobilize workers effectively and on the economic position of the industry.

The fact that unions are likely to use comparable worth as a recruiting tool does not prove that it helps or hurts overall economic efficiency or equity. We know of no evidence to settle this issue. In the absence of such evidence, we see no reason for action by legislatures or the courts to discourage unions from pursuing traditional goals that they feel can be advanced by relative wage adjustments based on comparable worth.

The broader use of comparable worth in setting wages depends on actions by government executives, Congress, and state and local legislatures, and on decisions by the courts.

Executive Action

Public-sector wages are now often set by job evaluation techniques. Furthermore, for good or ill, public-sector wage setting is inherently political; that is, wages are widely known and often reflect political priorities, and public-sector employment is sometimes used for patronage. While it might be preferable if such considerations played a smaller role in wage setting than they do, it is myopic to ignore them in setting policy. Moreover, in the current political climate only studied inattention to sex-based wage differences could prevent comparable worth from being considered in public-sector wage setting, both by government executives and by legislatures. There is no evidence that wage adjustments based on comparable worth would reduce overall efficiency in the public sector. Legislatures, city councils, city managers, and other elected or appointed officials could choose to implement comparable worth in the public sector without in any way requiring private-sector employers to do so. The example set in the

---

weights assigned to specific job attributes in job evaluations. Policemen and firemen in Minnesota, for example, have objected to inclusion in the state's job evaluation study on the ground that traditional job evaluation techniques give too little weight to hazards they routinely encounter. Workers in such jobs argue that separate job evaluation procedures should be used to measure correctly the worth of such jobs. *Wall Street Journal,* May 10, 1985.

57. Between 1929 and 1962, wage dispersion in selected occupations within the iron and steel industry narrowed by 50 to 75 percent. See Elbaum, "The Making and Shaping of Job and Pay Structures in the Iron and Steel Industry," pp. 91–93.

public sector would influence private-sector employers or unions, but would no more compel private emulation than public-sector pensions require private-sector employers to set up retirement plans.

Judicial and Legislative Action

The central issue for courts and legislatures regarding comparable worth concerns the role it should play in civil rights legislation and litigation. This branch of law is highly developed. If arguments based on comparable worth are to be used extensively in wage discrimination cases, they must fit within that framework.

Generally speaking, plaintiffs who wish to prove that they have suffered illegal discrimination may pursue either or both of two lines of argument.[58] First, they may argue that they have been victims of "disparate treatment." They establish a prima facie case if they can show that the disparate treatment is based on their race, religion, sex, or national origin. An example would be an employer's refusal to interview people because of their race or sex. If the defendant can show a legitimate business reason for the disparate treatment, then the burden of proof reverts to the plaintiffs to show that this justification is just a pretext for intentional discriminatory behavior.

Alternatively, the plaintiffs may argue that the actions of the defendant have had a "disparate impact" on them. This claim can be sustained only if the plaintiffs show that the disparate impact is suffered by a group distinguished by a "suspect classification," such as race, religion, or sex. To continue the example above, disparate impact would exist if the employer's refusal to interview people because of their race or sex led to the underrepresentation of that race or sex among the interviewer's employees. If the plaintiffs can establish a prima facie case that actions by the defendant have had a disparate and presumably harmful impact, then the burden of proof is on the defendant to show a business necessity—something he must do, for example, in order to stay in business. The court then weighs the business justification against the national interest in protecting the interests of the affected group.[59]

58. See Robert Lawrence Bragg, "Comparable Worth and Title VII: The Case Against Disparate Impact Analysis," *Pacific Law Journal*, vol. 16 (April 1985), pp. 833–51.

59. Ibid., p. 846.

The vital distinction between these two types of cases concerns the nature of the possible justification for the challenged business practice, which in turn determines which party must bear the burden of proof. In cases of disparate treatment, if the defendant can show his actions were legitimately related to his business, the burden is on the plaintiffs to show discriminatory intent. In cases of disparate impact, the defendant bears the burden of proof to show that his actions are necessary to his or her business. Clearly, the plaintiff—the person claiming to have suffered discrimination—has an easier time if the defendant must show that his behavior is necessary for business survival than if the plaintiff must show discriminatory intent by the defendant. The issue in wage discrimination cases is whether analyses based on comparable worth should be sufficient to establish a prima facie case of disparate impact, thus placing the burden of proof on the employer defendant.

A second issue concerns the circumstances in which the courts should entertain arguments that different wages constitute discrimination. The extremes are well established. No serious legal doubt exists that the Equal Pay Act outlaws unequal pay for identical work. This prohibition includes jobs different only in title or in characteristics judged to be superficial. In such situations, pay must be the same even if employers can find people willing to work for unequal pay. In fact, the purpose of the Equal Pay Act is to override market realities in such cases. On the other hand, no serious doubt exists that employers may give different pay to workers performing tasks that entail very different skills, risks, or working conditions where no group defined by a suspect classification is injured and no intent to discriminate exists; in such cases the verdict of the market is final. The question, therefore, is whether the protections now accorded under the Equal Pay Act to workers performing essentially identical jobs should be extended to workers performing jobs deemed similar according to some criteria.

Each of these questions is now at issue in many cases, and conflicting decisions have been rendered in various courts. Our purpose is not to resolve the interpretation of current law, but to suggest an approach either for the courts, if they deem it consistent with current law, or for Congress, if they do not.

By enacting the Equal Pay Act, title VII of the Civil Rights Act, and other measures to improve job access and pay of various groups, Congress has stated clearly that it is prepared to reject the verdict of the market in some situations. This legislation embodies the judgment that in some cases the market has generated and perpetuated discriminatory practices unacceptable to Congress. The view that such legislation should be rejected because it undermines the operation of the market has little support. For reasons suggested by our review of labor market theories, we think that Congress has been right to interfere with the unfettered operation of labor markets in these circumstances. On the other extreme, only a few radical critics of the market system are indifferent to nonmarket interference with wage setting. Decentralized decisionmaking in markets is prized for its contributions to both economic efficiency and political pluralism.

The practical question, therefore, concerns the circumstances under which the results of market transactions are sufficiently objectionable to warrant interference by the courts. This question hinges on the possible gains from interfering with market outcomes and the capacity of the courts to do so in a consistent manner. In the case of comparable worth, the practical question is whether a job evaluation that shows an unexplained difference between wages in jobs held predominantly by each sex should be treated by the courts as sufficient to establish a prima facie case of disparate impact. If job evaluations could establish a prima facie case of disparate impact, defendants would bear the burden of proof to establish that their actions producing such effects are a business necessity sufficiently important to override national interests in the well-being of the adversely affected group. However, if job evaluations were entirely excluded, plaintiffs would bear the burden of proof to show that defendants engaged intentionally in discriminatory behavior, a difficult case to prove.

We suggest that by themselves the results of job evaluations should not be regarded as sufficient to establish a prima facie case of disparate impact. Our reasons are practical. Job evaluations are widely used by private and public employers. A technology exists for comparing attributes of different jobs, calibrating these attributes with market wages, and correcting "outliers," jobs whose pay is out of line with pay of other jobs with similar characteristics. In situations that are not adversarial or where the issues dividing the parties are minor, this system helps to increase the sense of order and fairness associated with pay scales. There is no evidence on whether this use of job evaluations helps or hinders economic efficiency, but it is widely accepted by both labor and management.

However, in hotly contested situations, such as when one party accuses the other of wage discrimination, we do not believe that the courts are equipped to handle the myriad technical controversies that would arise over the use of job evaluations. The first problem concerns the circumstances under which a job evaluation would be admissible. Who would be permitted to sponsor an admissible job evaluation?

If anyone could commission a job evaluation admissible in establishing a prima facie case of disparate impact, large numbers of cases would probably result. Such a result would be unobjectionable, even salutary, if the results of any two evaluations were likely to be similar. Such convergence is unlikely. First, experts continue to disagree sharply over what variables are relevant in explaining pay differences. Second, even if the explanatory variables were not in dispute, analysts could employ many different mathematical forms, no one of which is demonstrably superior to the others. As indicated by the regressions described above, small variations in functional form, among which there is no rational basis for selection, can generate large differences in results. In short, courts would be asked to rest judgments in a huge number of cases almost entirely on highly technical issues on which experts cannot now or ever be expected to agree.

In many situations the courts must take on highly technical conflicting testimony of expert witnesses. The point being advanced here is not that the courts should shun statistical evidence; it is rather that they should not assume the burden of dealing with a large number of cases based on inherently ambiguous statistical analyses.

Numerous courts have vividly expressed their concern about their own incompetence to deal rationally and consistently with such disputes. For example, the Ninth Circuit Court of Appeals stated:

> Granting that statistics "when properly authenticated, constitute an accepted form of circumstantial evidence of discrimination," . . . we are still sobered by warnings that statistical evidence has an "inherently slippery nature" and "can be exaggerated, oversimplified, or distorted to create support for a position that is not otherwise supported by the evidence."[60]

The Fifth Circuit Court of Appeals even more vehemently expressed concern regarding the ability of the courts to interpret and weigh correctly the significance of statistical studies.

> In closing, we add a note both rueful and cautionary. The bar is reminded that sound statistical analysis is a task both complex and arduous. . . . We are no more statisticians than we are physicians, and counsel who

60. *Spaulding* v. *University of Washington*, 740 F.2d 686, 703 (9th Cir. 1984).

> expect of us informed and consistent treatment of such proofs are well advised to proceed as do those who advance knotty medical problems for resolution. . . . The day is long past . . . when we proceeded with any confidence toward broad conclusions from crude and incomplete statistics. That everyone who has eaten bread has died may tell us something about bread, but not very much.[61]

We have no doubt that selected judges are as capable as any professional statistician or economist in weighing conflicting claims in such disputes. We have just as little doubt that many judges are not. To illustrate the problem, we point to a recent article by Thomas J. Campbell that is meant to increase the sophistication of lawyers in handling statistical evidence by expert witnesses.[62] This article contains much helpful advice, but it also contains some seriously flawed suggestions. For example, Campbell holds that a statistically significant finding is undermined if it comes from a regression in which the independent variables explain only a small part of the variation of the dependent variable—in other words, from an equation with a low R^2.

This advice is not sound. In general, courts are trying to measure how one variable, X, influences another, Y. The influence of X on Y may be strong and the measurement may be statistically highly significant and dependably estimated even if the investigator can explain only a small part of the variation in Y. Much of the variation in Y may be attributable to factors on which data are not available or that would not alter the major finding under any reasonable expectation. Moreover, even if nearly all of the variation in Y is statistically explained—in other words, if the R^2 is near 1.0—the underlying relationship may be badly misspecified and the estimated coefficients may misrepresent the underlying relationships.

Good advice might be more nearly the opposite of what Campbell urges, at least in economics. The highest R^2s in economics, often 0.99 or larger, are produced from macroeconomic time series where, by common agreement, the estimated relationships are fragile and unreliable for policy purposes. In contrast, analyses of large cross-sectional data sets often yield highly reliable coefficients from equations in which 10 percent or less of the variance in the dependent variable can be

61. *Wilkins* v. *University of Houston*, 654 F.2d 388, 410 (5th Cir. 1981).

62. Thomas J. Campbell, "Regression Analysis in Title VII Cases: Minimum Standards, Comparable Worth, and Other Issues Where Law and Statistics Meet," *Stanford Law Review*, vol. 36 (July 1984), pp. 1299–1324, especially pp. 1309–11.

explained. The point is that a law journal as distinguished as the *Stanford Law Review* has published an article with the purpose of promoting statistical sophistication, but its effect would be to lead courts to commit fundamental errors in handling statistical evidence. Assigning a central role to job evaluations would put great stress on courts in an area they are not equipped to handle.

One suggestion some have made for dealing with this problem would be to treat as prima facie evidence of disparate impact the failure of an employer to adjust wages in response to a job evaluation that the *employer* commissioned and that indicated the presence of an unexplained gap in pay between men's and women's jobs. Such a rule would result in less litigation than one under which plaintiffs could commission job evaluations, but it suffers from two flaws. First, it might powerfully discourage employers from undertaking job evaluations in any situation where they fear possible suit from any employee. Second, although the scope for litigation would be reduced, the reliability of job evaluations in contested situations would not be improved.

For these reasons, we suggest that plaintiffs be permitted to submit job evaluation studies as part of their effort to establish a prima facie case of disparate treatment. The job evaluation studies should be subjected to "sensitivity analysis" to test for the robustness of any finding of a wage gap between men's and women's jobs.[63] That means that the estimated wage gap between men's and women's jobs should persist in equations expressed in different mathematical forms and including a wide range of plausible variables thought to have a legitimate influence on wage rates. If such a wage gap appears persistently, it should be taken as important evidence of disparate treatment, provided that it is corroborated by what Mary Becker has called the "smoldering background" of discriminatory practices—a collection of facts regarding employer practices, none of which is a "smoking gun" that establishes blatant discriminatory intent.[64] How much supporting evidence is required should depend on how similar the jobs are for which discriminatory wage setting is alleged. If the jobs are identical, the strictures of the Equal Pay Act prohibit unequal pay. If the jobs are similar but not

63. Edward E. Leamer, "Let's Take the Con Out of Econometrics," *American Economic Review*, vol. 73 (March 1983), pp. 31–43.

64. Mary E. Becker, "Comparable Worth in Antidiscrimination Legislation: A Reply to Freed and Polsby," *University of Chicago Law Review*, vol. 51 (Fall 1984), p. 1115, n. 17.

identical—orderlies and practical nurses, day and night shifts of the same job, for example—job evaluations would require only slight supplementation. But adjustments of pay for dissimilar jobs that are scored equally in job evaluation studies should require evidence of discriminatory intent as well as indications of disparate pay.

Such a procedure would preserve the relevance of arguments based on comparable worth in cases of wage discrimination. It would not permit a form of evidence that is relevant but inescapably ambiguous, if not supported by corroborating evidence, to force defendants either to justify current wage-setting practices as essential to the business's survival or to suffer judgment as a discriminatory employer. The courts have been following a procedure that closely resembles the one suggested here. We suggest that the continued admissibility of job evaluations be sanctioned, but limited.

Such an application of comparable worth would have little effect on overall economic efficiency, even if the fears of its opponents are solidly grounded. This conclusion is supported by the experience of Australia with wage adjustments similar to those that would follow from comparable worth. Whether the labor market effects of the Australian experiment with pay equalization were small or large, they suggest that the impact on demand for women in the labor market would be negligibly affected by the approach to comparable worth suggested here. We conclude that the economic side effects of the use of comparable worth that we recommend will be minor.

The economic gains also will be modest, however. Most of the gap between men's and women's wages would remain even if the principles of comparable worth were aggressively and widely applied. Equality for women in the labor market will require the use of other instruments for combating discrimination. Among these instruments are affirmative action under Executive Order 11246 of 1965. This order, as amended in 1974, requires federal contractors to "not discriminate against any employee or applicant for employment because of race, color, religion, sex, or national origin . . ." and to "take affirmative action to ensure that applicants are employed, and that employees are treated during employment, without regard to their race, color, religion, sex or national origin."[65] Another instrument is litigation under title VII of the Civil Rights Act of 1964. Title VII litigation has been most effective in

65. 3 C.F.R. 170 (1974).

increasing employment opportunities for blacks and other minorities, but it has also had a significant effect on the employment of women.[66]

Thus comparable worth should be seen as one instrument among several, crude and inexact, that should be used in situations where the facts and circumstances suggest its value. Against this background, it would be unfortunate if Congress or the courts tried to lay down neat rules for when it should be employed.

Appendix

Figures 2 and 3 are based on twenty regressions based on equations 1–5. We ran four versions of each equation as described below. The data that we used to estimate the parameters of each equation came from Helen Remick of the University of Washington.

The equations, with the estimated coefficients, are listed below. The independent variables are also defined. We then describe how we used these equations to obtain the data graphed in figures 2 and 3.

The variables in equations A-1 through A-20 are defined as follows:

S = actual salary for 117 occupations in the Washington State government;

JP = job evaluation points assigned to each job by Norman Willis and Associates;

D = a dummy variable that = 1 if at least 50 percent of the incumbents of a particular job are women and 0 if more than 50 percent are men;

66. Between 1967 and 1974, the effects of title VII and Executive Order 11246 as amended increased the likelihood of a woman being employed in a male-dominated occupation by 6.6 percent. See Andrea H. Beller, "Occupational Segregation by Sex: Determinants and Changes," *Journal of Human Resources,* vol. 17 (Summer 1982), p. 390. Jonathan Leonard confirms the positive impact of affirmative action on women's employment. He found that between 1974 and 1980 the share of white women in establishments subject to Executive Order 11246 grew 3.5 percent faster than it did in other establishments. Leonard's study reports that among females affirmative action increased the demand for blacks relative to whites by 11 percent. In terms of promoting occupational integration, Leonard found that affirmative action has contributed to the occupational advance of black females, but has had a mixed impact on white females. See Jonathan S. Leonard, "The Effectiveness of Equal Employment Law and Affirmative Action Regulation," National Bureau of Economic Research Working Paper 1745 (Cambridge, Mass.: NBER, October 1985), p. 13.

F = percentage of the incumbents of each job who are female;
F^* = F, unless none of the incumbents of a job are female, in which case the variable was set at 0.001.

The numbers in parentheses are t-statistics; the R^2s are all corrected.

(A-1)
$$S = \underset{(25.1)}{552.2} + \underset{(18.2)}{1.6}\,JP - \underset{(9.2)}{183.3}\,D$$
$$R^2 = 0.762$$

(A-2)
$$S = \underset{(25.5)}{561.3} + \underset{(18.6)}{1.6}\,JP - \underset{(9.5)}{2.1}\,F$$
$$R^2 = 0.770$$

(A-3)
$$S = \underset{(16.3)}{499.2} + \underset{(13.3)}{1.9}\,JP - \underset{(2.2)}{93.8}\,D - \underset{(2.4)}{0.4}\,JP \times D$$
$$R^2 = 0.772$$

(A-4)
$$S = \underset{(16.1)}{515.7} + \underset{(12.6)}{1.8}\,JP - \underset{(2.9)}{1.3}\,F - \underset{(1.9)}{0.004}\,JP \times F$$
$$R^2 = 0.775$$

(A-5)
$$S = \underset{(11.2)}{511.9} + \underset{(5.3)}{1.9}\,JP - \underset{(1.0)}{0.0006}\,(JP)^2 - \underset{(9.1)}{181.9}\,D$$
$$R^2 = 0.762$$

(A-6)
$$S = \underset{(11.7)}{530.3} + \underset{(5.1)}{1.9}\,JP - \underset{(0.8)}{0.0005}\,(JP)^2 - \underset{(9.4)}{2.1}\,F$$
$$R^2 = 0.769$$

(A-7)
$$S = \underset{(10.8)}{493.8} + \underset{(5.2)}{1.9}\,JP - \underset{(0.2)}{0.0001}\,(JP)^2$$
$$- \underset{(2.2)}{95.8}\,D - \underset{(2.2)}{0.4}\,JP \times D$$
$$R^2 = 0.770$$

(A-8)
$$S = 514.9 + \underset{(11.2)}{} 1.8\,JP \underset{(5.0)}{} - 0.00002\,(JP)^2 \underset{(0.02)}{}$$

$$- 1.3\,F - 0.004\,JP \times F$$

(11.2) (5.0) (0.02); (2.7) (1.8)

$R^2 = 0.773$

(A-9)
$$S = -1015.3 + 363.5 \ln(JP) - 177.7\,D$$

(9.3) (17.4) (8.6)

$R^2 = 0.745$

(A-10)
$$S = -1013.7 + 350.2 \ln(JP) - 17.5 \ln(F^*)$$

(8.8) (15.9) (7.4)

$R^2 = 0.715$

(A-11)
$$S = -1119.2 + 383.6 \ln(JP) + 13.8\,D$$

(6.9) (12.3) (0.06)

$$- 36.6 \ln(JP) \times D$$

(0.9)

$R^2 = 0.745$

(A-12)
$$S = -1052.4 + 357.8 \ln(JP) + 9.4 \ln(F^*)$$

(8.7) (15.5) (0.4)

$$- 5.1 \ln(JP) \times \ln(F^*)$$

(1.1)

$R^2 = 0.716$

(A-13)
$$\ln(S) = 4.5 + 0.4 \ln(JP) - 0.2\,D$$

(39.2) (19.6) (10.4)

$R^2 = 0.793$

(A-14)
$$\ln(S) = 4.5 + 0.4 \ln(JP) - 0.02 \ln(F^*)$$

(35.8) (17.3) (8.5)

$R^2 = 0.752$

(A-15)
$$\ln(S) = \underset{(26.7)}{4.6} + \underset{(12.8)}{0.4} \ln (JP) - \underset{(1.5)}{0.3}\, D + \underset{(0.5)}{0.02} \ln (JP) \times D$$
$$R^2 = 0.792$$

(A-16)
$$\ln(S) = \underset{(34.0)}{4.5} + \underset{(16.5)}{0.4} \ln (JP) - \underset{(0.6)}{0.02} \ln (F^*) - \underset{(0.2)}{0.0009} \ln (JP) \times \ln (F^*)$$
$$R^2 = 0.750$$

(A-17)
$$\ln(S) = \underset{(257.0)}{6.4} + \underset{(18.8)}{0.002}\, JP - \underset{(10.3)}{0.2}\, D$$
$$R^2 = 0.779$$

(A-18)
$$\ln(S) = \underset{(260.5)}{6.4} + \underset{(19.4)}{0.002}\, JP - \underset{(10.8)}{0.003}\, F$$
$$R^2 = 0.789$$

(A-19)
$$\ln(S) = \underset{(180.2)}{6.3} + \underset{(12.3)}{0.002}\, JP - \underset{(3.9)}{0.2}\, D - \underset{(1.1)}{0.0002}\, JP \times D$$
$$R^2 = 0.779$$

(A-20)
$$\ln(S) = \underset{(175.6)}{6.4} + \underset{(11.9)}{0.002}\, JP - \underset{(4.5)}{0.002}\, F - \underset{(0.7)}{0.000002}\, JP \times F$$
$$R^2 = 0.788$$

Each equation generated an estimate of the wage that would be paid to incumbents of each type of job based on the number of job evaluation points and the sex of the incumbent. The variables indicating the sex composition of the incumbents are necessary to detect whether jobs held predominantly by one sex are paid systematically different wages from jobs with similar job-point scores held by the other sex.

We calculated the estimated wage for each job based on each equation. To this estimate we added (or subtracted, depending on the sign of the coefficient) an amount so that the wage was the same as it would have been if all workers were male. We then calculated the percentage deviation of this estimated wage from the actual wage.

For example, incumbents of job number 19 received a salary of $1,587.00 per month. The job was assigned 562 job points, and it was filled predominantly by women ($D = 1$). The natural logarithm of that wage is 7.3696. Based on equation A-19 with the coefficients unrounded, the natural logarithm estimated wage for an occupation with 562 job points filled predominantly by women is: $6.345 + 0.00198(562) - 0.1858(1) - 0.00022(562)(1) = 7.14832$. Removing the systematic difference between predominantly female and predominantly male jobs involves offsetting, or adding back, the third and fourth terms and yields 7.45776, the natural logarithm of the wage of a job with 562 job points filled predominantly by men, or $1,733.26. To reach this wage the actual wage must be increased 9.2 percent: $[(1{,}733.26 - 1{,}587.00) \div (1{,}587.00)] \times 100$.

Index

HD6061.2.U6 A[illegible]7 1986 c.1
Aaron, Henry J. cn 100106 000
The comparable worth controver
3 9310[illegible] 00074329 2
GOSHEN COLLEGE-GOOD LIBRARY